# GHOSTS

## *of the*

# WORLD

## True Tales of Ghostly Hauntings

## Susan Smitten

LONE
PINE

Lone Pine Publishing International

© 2006 by Lone Pine Publishing International Inc.
First printed in 2006 10 9 8 7 6 5 4 3 2 1
Printed in Canada

**The Publisher: Lone Pine Publishing International**
Distributed by Lone Pine Publishing
1808 B Street NW, Suite 140
Auburn, WA 98001
USA

**Websites:** www.lonepinepublishing.com
www.ghostbooks.net

**National Library of Canada Cataloguing in Publication Data**

Smitten, Susan, 1961-
  Ghosts of the world: true tales of ghostly hauntings / Susan Smitten.

  ISBN-13: 978-1-894877-65-7
  ISBN-10: 1-894877-65-9

  1. Ghosts. I. Title.

GR580.S677 2006          133.1          C2006-900465-X

*Photo Credits:* Every effort has been made to accurately credit photographers. Any errors or omissions should be directed to the publisher for changes in future editions. The photographs and illustrations in this book are reproduced with the kind permission of the following sources: Castle of Spirits.com (p. 150, 168, 171, 173, 182); Dragsholm Slot (p. 47, 186); Fairmont Hotel Vancouver (p. 134); Istock (p. 14, 55: Jeremy Voisey, p. 85, 87: Michael Mory); Laird of Balgonie (pp. 4–5, p. 16, 21); Library of Congress (p. 43: USZ62-68664; p. 65: USZC4-4767; p. 67, 70: HABS DC,WASH,134-292; p. 83: USZ62-128730; p. 128: HABS AK,8-JUNE,6-1; p. 148: USZ62-25833); Minnesota Historical Society (p. 213, 217: 40765); Monte Cristo Homestead (p. 97, 116, 137, 140); Princess Theater (p. 222); Scottish Paranormal Investigations/Brodick Castle/National Trust for Scotland (p. 29, 31).

PC: P5

For my niece Charlotte

for Kathy, KT, Lynda and Maureen –
for times shared, a decade of laughter and tears

*The possible's slow fuse is lit, by the Imagination.*
*— Emily Dickinson*

# Contents

Acknowledgments 6

Introduction 8

## Chapter One: Castles

Green Jeanie of Balgonie NEAR MARKINCH, FIFE, SCOTLAND 15

Berry Pomeroy Castle TOTNES, DEVON, ENGLAND 24

Brodick Castle ISLE OF ARRAN, SCOTLAND 28

Tragedy in Chillingham NORTHUMBERLAND, ENGLAND 33

The Diva Lives On BRECON BEACONS NATIONAL PARK, WALES 40

Dragsholm Slot HØRVE, ZEALAND ISLAND, DENMARK 46

Great Glamis! FORFAR, TAYSIDE, SCOTLAND 52

Ruthin Castle DENBIGHSHIRE, WALES 60

Salzburg Castle SALZBURG, AUSTRIA 64

## Chapter Two: Government & Public Places

Banished! NIAMEY, NIGER 68

Ghosts at the White House WASHINGTON, DC, USA 69

Phantom Menace or Presidential Scam? LILONGWE, MALAWI 74

Sao Paulo City Hall SAO PAULO, BRAZIL 76

Terror in the Tunisian Embassy MOSCOW, RUSSIA 78

The Kremlin's Terrible Ghost MOSCOW, RUSSIA 82

Visions at Versailles PARIS, FRANCE 86

Dalkeith Fire Station DALKEITH, LOTHIAN, SCOTLAND 93

Middlesbrough Ambulance Station
MIDDLESBROUGH, NORTH YORKSHIRE, ENGLAND 95

## Chapter Three: Homes

No. 12 Deanery Lane PIETERMARITZBURG, KWAZULA-NATAL, SOUTH AFRICA 98

Plas Teg PONTBLYDDYN, NEAR MOLD, FLINTSHIRE, WALES 100

The White Lady of Samlesbury Hall PRESTON, LANCASHIRE, ENGLAND 105

The White Witch of Rose Hall MONTEGO BAY, JAMAICA 110

## Chapter Four: Hotels & Inns

England's Most Haunted House?
WOTTON-UNDER-EDGE, GLOUCESTERSHIRE, ENGLAND 117

Cecil Plains Homestead DARLING DOWNS, QUEENSLAND, AUSTRALIA 123
Ghosts, Not Gold, in the Alaskan Hotel JUNEAU, ALASKA, USA 127
The Lady in Red VANCOUVER, BRITISH COLUMBIA, CANADA 132
Monte Cristo Homestead JUNEE, NEW SOUTH WALES, AUSTRALIA 136
Phantom in Franschhoek FRANSCHHOEK, SOUTH AFRICA 144
Yun Shan Fan Dian Hotel CHENGDE, CHINA 147

## Chapter Five: Odd Places

Cricket, Anyone? PIETERMARITZBURG, KWAZULA-NATAL, SOUTH AFRICA 151
Ghost Mountain KWAZULA-NATAL, SOUTH AFRICA 152
Ghost Planes of Derbyshire SHEFFIELD, SOUTH YORKSHIRE, ENGLAND 156
Pluckley's Many Phantoms PLUCKLEY, KENT, ENGLAND 160
Quarantine Station SYDNEY, NEW SOUTH WALES, AUSTRALIA 167

## Chapter Six: Prisons

Haunted "Hell on Earth" PORT ARTHUR, TASMANIA 174
Oakalla Prison Phantoms BURNABY, BRITISH COLUMBIA, CANADA 178
The Old Melbourne Gaol MELBOURNE, VICTORIA, AUSTRALIA 181

## Chapter Seven: Pubs & Restaurants

Dick Whittington's Pub GLOUCESTER, GLOUCESTERSHIRE, ENGLAND 187
The Greyhound Inn LINGFIELD, SURREY, ENGLAND 190
Visiting the Wheatsheaf THORNTON HEATH, SURREY, ENGLAND 192
The Castleview Pub AYRSHIRE, SCOTLAND 195
Culcreuch Castle STIRLINGSHIRE, SCOTLAND 196

## Chapter Eight: Roads

George's Hill CALVERTON, NOTTINGHAM, ENGLAND 200
Highway Sheila DURBAN, KWAZULU-NATAL, SOUTH AFRICA 202
Go, Go, Go, Ghost Car! CAPE TOWN, WESTERN CAPE, SOUTH AFRICA 205
Roadside Wraiths: Scotland's Haunted A75 DUMFRIESSHIRE, SCOTLAND 207

## Chapter Nine: Theaters

Dressing Room No. 9 DUBLIN, IRELAND 214
The Mounds Theatre ST. PAUL, MINNESOTA, USA 216
The Phantom "Federici" MELBOURNE, VICTORIA, AUSTRALIA 221
The Tron Theatre GLASGOW, SCOTLAND 225

# Acknowledgments

There are many people to thank for their contributions to this book. I especially wish to thank Raeann Ruth for sharing her incredible experiences at the Mounds Theatre. The Laird of Balgonie and Eddergoll, Raymond Morris, provided me with wonderful stories and an extensive history of Balgonie Castle. I am thankful to Craig Rutherfoord at the Ghost Mountain Inn who went above and beyond to fax me information at all hours in order to cope with the time zone differences. I want to extend my gratitude to Glennis Philby, Scott Fry, Jim Davidson, Reg and Olive Ryan, Kirsten Rasmussen, Lesley Dennis, Sir Humphrey, Stacy Jones and Ada Donaldson for sharing their amazing stories and insights.

I owe many thanks to David Smith of Scottish Paranormal Investigations for sharing his research on several locations including Brodick Castle and the Tron Theatre. Special thanks to Jo Holness of UK Paranormal for providing copies of her investigations at the Ancient Ram Inn and the Greyhound Inn. I am very grateful to Derek Green and the Ghost Club for assisting with my research in Scotland. I want to thank Rowena Gilbert of Australia's Castle of Spirits.com for her ongoing support and for providing much of the information on the ghosts down under. I also owe my thanks to Dennis William Hauck, author of many splendid books and creator of the Haunted Places newsletter, which allowed me to connect to some of the people in this book. Similarly, I want to extend my thanks to Jeff Belanger for access to his Ghost Village web site.

And finally, I would be nothing without the incredible team at Lone Pine Publishing. My heartfelt thanks go to Shane Kennedy, Nancy Foulds, Carol Woo and Trina Koscielnuk.

# Introduction

Here is what I learned in writing about the ghosts that populate our world. The number of places across this planet that are haunted is almost infinite—and always changing—as some places acquire ghosts while others lose theirs. Virtually every city, castle, famous building, theater, prison, battlefield and dark country road has its associated ghosts and any attempt to describe them all would be frustrating and futile. What I have collected here is an eclectic mix of some of the more famous ghosts and some of the newer, lesser-known ghosts that make life interesting for those who share their space.

It is abundantly clear that for all our differences the world over, we as humans commune regularly with ghosts. Call them what you will—*bhut* in India, *domovoy* in Russia, *bansidhe* in Ireland and Scotland, *forso* in New Guinea or *yurei* in Japan—the existence of paranormal phenomena thrives in almost every culture. After all, next to birth, the most universal aspect of being human is dealing with death.

Archaeological digs reveal that our prehistoric ancestors buried their dead with jewelry, weapons, tools and other votive items on the assumption that the innate qualities possessed by humans while living were eternal. Aware that after death the physical form decays and ultimately ceases to exist, the other eternal qualities had to take on a separate form, which became known as the spirit or soul. The belief was that this separate spiritual form, once released from the earthbound body, was transported to another place. This idea is universal to all cultures; however, there are myriad

interpretations and manipulations ranging from spirit entities that never had a material form, such as angels, to the
notion that everything from amethyst to zephyr lilies has a
spirit. But it's not enough to set up this belief structure. To
become permanently ingrained as part of our human culture, the spirit had to take a material form and *reveal* itself.
As a result, ghost sightings have been reported throughout
recorded history.

The oldest religions and some of humanity's oldest writings contain references to contact with demons, gods and the
spirits of the dead. In Homer's *Iliad*, Achilles is visited by
the soul of his warrior friend Patroclus who asks that he be
properly cremated and also warns Achilles of his death during the final battle at Troy. In the 5th century BC there is
Herodotus' tale of how Periander, the tyrant of Corinth,
received a visit by the soul of his dead wife in order to help
him find a missing object. It was said that the infamous
Roman emperor Caligula haunted the Lamian Gardens
until his ashes were properly interred. Greek philosopher
Athenodorus had the unfortunate luck to rent a house in the
1st century AD that was haunted by a ghost in chains. The
ghost led Athenodorus to a site in the garden where his
bones had been roughly buried still shackled, and after the
philosopher gave the skeleton a decent burial the ghost never
returned. You get the point.

Jump ahead to the 21st century. According to a Harris
public opinion poll conducted in January 2003, more than
half of the American population of the United States believes
in ghosts. Some polls suggest that at least 50 percent of the
world's population supports the notion of ghosts and a full
third claims to have seen one. The recent surge in interest in

the paranormal, with dozens of new organizations forming to investigate cases and media getting on the bandwagon with a deluge of programs and articles about the subject, suggests people are no longer pretending this phenomenon does not exist. And though the belief in ghosts is flourishing, as I mentioned there are countless cultural variations on exactly what ghosts are and why they appear.

Traditional European cultures embrace ghosts as the conscious spirit essence of someone who has died but may be unable to pass on to the spirit realms because there are unfinished tasks on Earth, or because the person refuses to believe he or she is dead. In Chinese and other Asian cultures, a human being has two souls, the *kwei*, or earth-soul, which remains on earth and eventually fades, and the divine soul, considered to be the true living essence and which returns home to the spiritual realm after death. The *kwei* or earth-soul is what many would call a ghost, although it is not believed to be the essence of the person but rather a sort of crude copy. Experts in the paranormal theorize that these ghosts have no connection to spirit at all but are a type of impression left behind by a person, much like a video recording that is stuck on replay. (In fact, they're often called "replay ghosts"—more on that later.) This type of phenomena is both repetitious and purposeless, as there is no hidden message or ability to contact or connect with the living.

To the layperson, the term ghost is interchangeable with many other words that may or may not mean the same thing. Popular culture uses words such as apparition, spirit, shade, poltergeist, phantom and entity to describe virtually identical occurrences. Although the stories in this book come from different cultures, they are amazingly similar in their basic characteristics. Whatever you choose to call them, ghosts have the ability to affect all the senses, presenting as a sound, a smell, an image, a touch, a feeling of intense cold, a sensation of intruding presence or all of the above. Parapsychologists postulate that apparitions—the temporarily visible forms of ghosts—are the result of absorbing energy or matter from the immediate surroundings. Many people will complain of feeling cold after being in contact with a ghost, and there are countless tales of camera batteries draining in minutes as the ghost swiped the energy from them. Another theory I read about is that apparitions are more in line with an hallucination, but one that is controlled by the ghost. The notion has been put forward that ghosts can actually stimulate the visual centers of the brain in some unknown fashion. It's a little out there, but who knows? If there is one thing that is clear, there are more things going on in this universe than meet the eye. Animals, with their keener senses, are believed to have the ability to see or sense the presence of ghosts when humans perceive nothing unusual.

One of the key distinctions made between types of ghosts is inanimate versus animate. You have likely heard the tale of the Flying Dutchman, where the captain and crew went down with a ship near the Cape of Good Hope during a vicious squall and were said to be doomed to sail the seas for eternity. A ghostly ship appears during raging storms, and it is generally a bad omen for those who witness it. It is also a classic tale of an inanimate phantom—an object that somehow returns to haunt this land of the living even though it was never alive, and the manifestation does not interact with observers aside from being seen or heard.

Reports of phantom cars, bridges and even telephone booths fall into this category as well.

Animate phantoms, it seems obvious to state, are the ghosts of former living creatures—human or otherwise. Some of these ghosts appear to be completely unaware of their surroundings, walking through walls and never interacting with their environment. These are the "replay" ghosts, repeating some action as if they are a film being projected and are caught in an eternal loop, playing over and over. The reason they walk through walls is that during the time when they lived, there was probably a door or opening in their path, but because they are just images without conscious qualities, they do not perceive any change to their route. One theory is that the actual surroundings, such as stone, wood, water and even air, have absorbed the images and somehow play them back. Then there are the sentient ghosts, animate phantoms that display some form of consciousness, which includes trying to communicate, moving objects, turning lights on and off, closing or opening doors, whispering in your ear, that sort of thing. Just ask the staff at the Tron Theatre in Scotland or Reg and Olive Ryan at Australia's Monte Cristo about living with sentient specters! Why do they haunt their location? That depends on whom you ask. Some people believe ghosts are tied to this place by either a traumatic death, an unbreakable emotional tie or some sense of commitment. Others postulate that ghosts may hang around simply because they loved a place so much they refuse to leave.

Other anomalies that should be mentioned are orbs and vortexes, balls and streaks of light that often show up on digital cameras and are the bane of the skeptic's existence—most such incidents are written off as light flares or dust particles. However, odd things are captured on film and are hard to explain away, and quite frankly it is hard to tell what these things are. They may not be spirits at all. They could be natural phenomenon we have not been able to detect yet, or the result of faulty equipment used to capture their image. Or they could be evidence of a spirit, a manifestation of some type of energy that wants us to know it is out there.

So come along for a little journey through the eeriest places on Earth. Be an armchair traveler and hike up a haunted mountain in South Africa, wander through ghost-filled castles in Scotland, meet the household spirits at an Australian B & B, and marvel at the many presidential ghosts popping up at the White House. Because even if you don't believe in ghosts, they have a way of capturing the imagination. Ghosts are ancient, mythic. They are part of our DNA. And the truth is there's nothing like a good ghost story. Enjoy!

# 1
# Castles

# Green Jeanie of Balgonie
## Near Markinch, Fife, Scotland

They call her Green Jeanie and for good reason. The ghost for which Balgonie Castle is most famous is "pea green in colour." Her verdant image has roamed the 14th-century sandstone structure in Fife, Scotland for more than 200 years, accompanied by an eclectic collection of spirits that include a gray man, a man's head and collar that float around the first floor, a ghostly dog and a 17th-century soldier.

The current Laird of Balgonie and Eddergall, Raymond Morris, his wife Margaret (Lady of Balgonie) and their son Stuart (the Younger Balgonie) have a long list of strange experiences to share since moving into the castle in 1985. "Between the three of us, we've seen at least 10 figures in the 20 years that we've lived here and they are usually green, gray or white," says the Laird. "It's a happy castle. They never bother us." The Laird has seen the least of the ghosts, with his wife experiencing the most. He surmises she may have inherited the gift of "second sight" from her Stewart ancestry. They have all seen Green Jeanie—or the Green Lady as they call her—mainly in the Great Hall. That is where the bulk of the supernatural goings-on take place. Her skin is a pale green color but they can't distinguish any features of her face because she wears a hooded cape. Of course, they had heard the stories of the green wraith that walked the dark halls of Balgonie, but that really didn't bother them when they bought the derelict structure. They had more pressing concerns, like the moss growing up the inner walls.

*The tower, built for Sir Thomas Sibbald of Balgonie, is regarded as one of the finest in Scotland.*

Prior to Raymond Morris' purchase, the hauntingly lovely five-story tower building sat completely empty, abandoned by its owner. It was a sad state unbefitting a castle that hosted such prestigious guests as Mary Queen of Scots and James IV, and was the seat for the Earls of Leven for many years. Other famous visitors include Rob Roy MacGregor who stayed in the garrison in 1716 with 200 clansmen and 20 Hanoverian prisoners. The 75-foot sandstone tower, built for Sir Thomas Sibbald, the King's Treasurer, in 1360, is the oldest standing structure in Fife and is regarded as one of the finest in the country. Additions were made to the castle in the three centuries that followed, with the construction of the final wing in 1702 by the 3rd Earl of Leven. But by 1840, the ghosts pretty much had free run of the place. In fact, the first reports of "Green Jeanie" appear in 1842, describing her as a "well-known phantom." As for the castle, locals had taken to writing to the Edinburgh newspapers about the appalling condition of Balgonie. In the 1950s, to avoid paying a roof tax the owners at the time went so far as to take the roofs off, making it open season for vandals and vagrants. There was an owner just prior to Raymond Morris who began restoring Balgonie but gave up when his wife's patience ran out. "It's not the life for everyone," mused the Laird in our interview. Neither is taking on a castle full of ghosts, but that didn't deter him or his family, who are the first to live in Balgonie in 160 years. "We live in the tower," explained the Laird. "The Great Hall on the first floor is the most haunted of all the rooms. It's where all the activity would have been during the castle's livelier days. And now, at night, we just close the doors because if you do go in there, you get the distinct feeling that it is occupied."

The ghosts didn't appear all at once. It took two or three years for them all to show themselves. The Younger Laird, Stuart, saw a white figure in 17th-century tights running through the Great Hall. He also witnessed the rather shocking vision of a man's head and collar float through the hall. "Not someone who had been beheaded," the Laird quickly clarified. "Just a ghost that only presents its head." Since most paranormal experts agree that ghosts require a tremendous amount of energy to manifest as an apparition visible to living eyes, perhaps this ghost uses just enough to let everyone know he is there.

The Laird's wife has seen the majority of the castle's spirits, and more often than the rest of the family. Margaret Morris observed the green visage of "Jeanie" when letting the family deerhounds out at 2 AM. She often sees her walk from left to right between two of the castle rooms that have an adjoining doorway. The Laird has also seen this phenomenon. "It's always the same. She never walks the other way, and she always stops to look through the second window into the courtyard."

It was the Lady of Balgonie who first saw the gray ghost of an old man that frequents the castle. She was resting in an armchair in the Laird's Hall, where the Morris family lives one floor above the Great Hall, and she opened her eyes to see a goatee-wearing apparition standing just 10 feet away. The Lady and the ghost stared at each other for several moments before he vanished. This ghost is one of the few to which they can put a name. "Alexander Leslie," says the Laird. His wife had enough time to study the man's face and remember it. When she later saw a portrait of Alexander Leslie, she told her husband that this was the same man who had appeared. That certainly fits with the castle's history. Sir Leslie bought the castle in 1635. According to the Balgonie Castle web site, Leslie served in the Swedish Army under King Gustavus Adolphus, rising to the rank of Field Marshal before his retirement in 1638. In 1641, Charles I raised him to a peerage with the titles of Earl of Leven and Lord Balgonie. He died in the castle at age 81. Apparently, he has spent the last 350 years or so roaming its halls, likely going gray at seeing his home slide into such a terrible state of disrepair.

Among the other apparitions, there is a soldier who is occasionally seen in the courtyard, a man dressed in medieval clothing, and a phantom dog. The Laird has been taken in by the canine ghost a couple of times, mistaking it for one of his three deerhounds. "I would hear the sound of a dog and go to the door to let it in, only there would be nothing there. I would then see my three dogs lying inside on the floor." Interestingly, his dogs are not affected by the ghosts. "They're not the smartest creatures," says the Laird with a note of humor.

There are other signs of spectral activity within Balgonie Castle. The Morrises hear whisperings or full conversations, mainly in the Great Hall, but never clearly enough to make out what is being said. They can usually discern what seems to be two men, two women or a man and woman. The Laird says he doubts he would understand them even if he could hear the speakers clearly because the ancient dialects are like a foreign language. And they have picked up on a distinct smell on a staircase that dates to 1666. "All of us are anti-smokers," he pointed out. "We have smelled very strong pipe tobacco on the stairs. It doesn't happen very often, I think the last time was six months ago, but it's quite obvious, strong and sweet."

There is only one example of someone being touched by a ghost in Balgonie. To help with restoration costs, the Laird rents some of the castle for weddings and banquets. One night in 1996, a waitress setting tables in the Great Hall for dinner felt someone brush by her back. She turned to look and no one was there.

With so many strange occurrences, the castle draws in plenty of people wanting to document the ghosts. The Laird obliges, happy to get the reports. His only stipulation is that they be out by 3 AM. "That's my bedtime." Scottish Paranormal Investigations explored the castle and courtyard in 2003, but didn't record much in the way of activity other than some general feelings of otherworldly presences. The group was on its first-ever outing, however, and plans to return soon because they admit they likely missed things owing to inexperience. The Ghost Club conducted an investigation in February 2005; members reported that the evening "proved to be very interesting and it seems fair to say that there is a general impression of activity, both smaller and larger scale." The investigators had a range of experiences from seeing shadows and orbs to hearing strange "thuds and bangs." One of the team claimed to see a cowled monk-like figure in the chapel moving in the back pew area. Two others felt something touch their ankles while in the Great Hall. Ghost Club investigator Derek Green told me, "Balgonie was a good night, as from the start of the investigation it was felt by a number of the team that the building had a definite strange atmosphere surrounding it, even the grounds outside the wall had a very strange feel to them. I did

*The Great Hall is the most haunted of all the rooms in the castle.*

immediately feel that something or someone was there. Sometimes when you walk into a location you do not feel the atmosphere, and you really have a feeling of emptiness." Green admits it is difficult to gather "conclusive proof" even with all their experience and equipment. But they work hard to eliminate all possible earth-bound explanations for the occurrences, and in Derek's opinion Balgonie Castle is haunted. "I do feel that what they are seeing could be genuine, as many reports of the ghosts of Balgonie over the years are detailed and documented very much the same. When reading about the sightings that cover over 100 years there does appear to be corroboration."

The Laird also invited a specialist in telluric energy to visit the castle. Telluric energy is said to be naturally occurring earth energy, which often travels in distinct paths called ley lines. Some liken it to the earth's "nervous system." Medieval alchemists implied that telluric current contained all the power necessary to create, transform and transmute all the materials of the entire planet. According to the alchemists, this energy was spiritual in content and was only found at certain specific ground control points, as with stone circles. David R. Cowan believes that cracks in the earth allow some of that energy to escape to the planet's surface and, depending on which of the energies is released, it creates good or bad energy that affects the health of those living above the cracks. Radiation, for example, is bad. In Cowan's report to the Laird, he rated the castle's energy system as healthy. "This surprised me," Cowan wrote, "since I expected ghosts (if that is what they were) to be initiated by unhealthy spirals. There was a spiral of healthy energy where the Green Lady had been seen and also another spiral in the baronial hall where the whisperings had been heard, with another in the old keep. These took the form of part of a semi-curve. With an unusual flash of inspiration, I could see it as a circle of spirals!"

In the courtyard Cowan found a pile of boulders that had been taken out of the old well, and he concluded that the builders of the castle knew enough to take telluric energy into account when planning the structure. "This must have been to give a healthy living environment to the occupants." Cowan told the Laird that similar to other centers of this type of energy, such as Winchester Cathedral, the Balgonie well became a pivotal point for a star-shaped network of energy that radiates outward. Those who live within range of these healthy vibes receive the direct benefit. "The Laird and his family were obviously responding to the healthy energies in their castle. Despite the inadequate heating facilities they were hale and hearty, and had never felt so healthy in their lives."

The Laird confirmed this information with me, saying they keep the castle unheated for the most part, and only heat their living quarters in the evening. It's apparently a lot like living with ghosts. "You get used to it," he said. "We've never been healthier."

There was one other interesting bit of information that David Cowan shared with the Laird and his family regarding the various colors of their ghostly gang. The green, gray and white tones are common to apparitions, and the theory put forward by psychic researcher Tom Lethbridge is that the ghosts originally appeared in the full spectrum of colors but over the centuries faded to one shade, the same way a multi-hued tapestry bleaches to white when exposed to the light for too long.

The Laird told me that the chapel is one of the busiest places in the castle now—not for ghosts but for getting married. They've had more than 800 weddings and only a few brides have been scared away by the thought of an uninvited spectral bridesmaid. "One of our first ministers wanted to exorcise them, but I said 'No way.' They don't bother us, so why would I?" So, if you are in Fife, you are cordially invited by the Laird to visit his abode and view his eternal house-guests. Just don't plan to stay overnight.

# Berry Pomeroy Castle
## TOTNES, DEVON, ENGLAND

A crumbling, isolated ruin perched on a wooded hill over-looking the River Dart makes a delightful location for a ghost story. After all, tales of ghosts and hauntings abound in Britain, and nearly every castle and stately home has its resident ghost, generally relating to some tragic event in its history. Why should Devon's Berry Pomeroy Castle be an exception? This place must be one of the most picked over, investigated and thoroughly examined ghost sites in the country. It is a wonder the spirits stick around for such scrutiny, yet stick around they do, and while they're at it, they create freak winds and cold spots, fire off guns and grab people when they least expect it.

The two main ghosts are color-coded; they are simply known as the White Lady and the Blue Lady. Though the names seem generic, both wraiths are directly connected to the castle's ancestry. A little history about the Berry Pomeroy will assist with a sense of context for these tragic stories. In 1066, the Pomeroy family began building the immense structure on land bestowed upon them by William the Conqueror—a little thank you for their loyalty during the Norman Invasions. The grand gatehouse and castle wall date from the end of the 13th century, and they surround the remains of a huge, flamboyant, somewhat incongruous mansion that was built within the confines of the Norman castle by the powerful Seymour family. The Seymours bought or somehow acquired the castle from the Pomeroy family in 1547. They wanted a more luxurious home so they created the "inner" structure in a very different style from the original castle. The two distinct architectural styles are obvious, even in today's state of ruin. By the late 17th century, the Seymours abandoned Berry Pomeroy. It was left to decay, and much of the castle burned in a mid-18th century fire. Eventually, English Heritage assumed responsibility for maintenance of the castle and in 1977 began restoration. Although a lot of work has gone into preventing further decay, visitors say nothing seems to remove the sense of foreboding, malaise, fear—even evil, which permeates the atmosphere.

Back to the ghosts. The White Lady is believed to be the spirit of Lady Margaret Pomeroy. Most ghost stories have many versions, but this legend tends to always be told the same way. Lady Margaret fell prey to her older, jealous (and apparently less attractive) sister Eleanor. As mistress of the castle, Eleanor wielded the power, an unfortunate thing for the lovely Margaret. When Eleanor fell in love with the same man as her younger sister, she took steps to remove the competition by having Margaret imprisoned in the dungeon that is now called St. Margaret's Tower. Not content to lock her rival away, the wicked Eleanor left Margaret to starve to death. It is not clear from the legend if this tactic worked to secure Eleanor a husband, but it did provide the castle with an ominous specter. The terrifying apparition of a white female figure is said to rise from St. Margaret's Tower (to the right of the main gate in the north corner) to the castle ramparts, beckoning to people. Her image is not one to be witnessed casually, because it is said anyone who sees her is about to die. Whether one takes that to be true or not, it is possible that after such a horrible, painful death, Lady Margaret's spirit contributes to the sense of anguish and fear that psychics or sensitives claim to feel whenever they visit the ruins.

The Blue Lady is a ghost with some variation to her story. Some reports claim she wanders about the castle grounds dressed in a long, blue cape, crying and looking for her dead child. Others say she is a portent of death—though that seems to be particular to the Seymour family. And still other tales claim she lures men to their death by appealing to them for help in dangerous parts of the castle. Her spirit dates back to the very early days of the castle. As the story goes, she was the daughter of one of the Norman lords and was raped and impregnated by her father. Some tales suggest the father strangled the child at birth in one of the castle's upper rooms; other versions make her the baby's killer, unable to look upon a child conceived incestuously. Either way, she continues to haunt Berry Pomeroy, an anguished soul still suffering. This story gained credibility after Sir Walter Farquhar, a physician attending the wife of one of the Stewards, witnessed the blue-robed spirit in the early 19th century. One account states that he saw a woman moving up the stairs, wringing her hands as if upset. Unaware of the ghost legend, he asked his patient's husband who the figure was, only to be told the apparition was a death omen. Dr. Farquhar dismissed the notion, assuring the man that his wife was on the mend and would recover; however, she inexplicably died soon after.

Moving to modern-day sightings, paranormal groups and tourists alike claim to have experienced many strange phenomena at Berry Pomeroy. Experiences include seeing odd lights, hearing voices and having cameras and equipment that malfunction while on site only to work fine later, which apparently happened to a BBC crew filming at the castle. According to a member of the Ghost Club Society who visits Berry Pomeroy frequently, the couple who runs the castle teashop has had a few weird experiences, from seeing a male-shaped shadow lurking outside the men's washroom to being grabbed on the shoulder by an invisible hand. There are reports of a blue light that emanates from St. Margaret's Tower on one specific night every year, although I was unable to ascertain which evening in particular. Other witnesses claim to have seen a human figure standing in one of the castle's top windows—something very supernatural because there are no longer any floors in the upper levels on which to stand.

The Torbay Investigators of the Paranormal (TIP), set up in 1995 by founder members David Phillips, Adrian Lodge and David Brown, state that in their experience, Berry Pomeroy Castle is "a clear No. 1 in the Devon ghosts chart." According to David Phillips, "I've had experiences there, of hearing gunfire and muskets going off. There are so many stories of ghosts and unexplained things going on there, it's got to be the most haunted building in Devon."

So if you are in the mood for a romantic ruin with a twist, be sure to make a trip to Totnes. The historic value may outweigh the haunted...but then again, perhaps not.

# Brodick Castle
## ISLE OF ARRAN, SCOTLAND

Eight hundred years of history are packed into the stately sandstone Brodick Castle on the Isle of Arran. It started out as a Viking fort and has been a stronghold since the 5th century. With its position on the bay commanding the approach to the Firth of Clyde, it was vital to controlling most of southern Scotland. The current castle dates from the mid to late 13th century when the Stewarts of Menteith built it. You would be hard-pressed, however, to envision what that original castle looked like standing over the north side of Brodick Bay, because it has been destroyed and rebuilt and extended nearly half a dozen times during its turbulent history. Most of what is visible today is part of a huge alteration started in 1844 by the 10th Duke of Hamilton and his wife, Princess Marie of Baden, doubling the castle's size. One aspect, however, that has been a constant for several generations now is its ghosts. There are at least two specters within Brodick Castle, and an unusual harbinger of death is said to roam the grounds.

Although, as mentioned, the current castle dates from about 1266, it underwent major alterations in 1544, 1588, 1652 and 1844. It was damaged mainly in violent battles, either between the English and Scottish or between the clans. The castle and the Earldom of Arran were held by the Hamilton family from 1503 when James IV granted the land to his cousin Lord Hamilton. In 1616 one of his descendents became the 1st Duke of Hamilton; his life came to a rather sudden end when he was tried and beheaded just months

*An unusual harbinger of death is said to roam the grounds at Brodick Castle.*

after being taken prisoner by Cromwell's soldiers during the Second Civil War in 1648. The Earldom of Arran died out in about 1575, with the insane 3rd earl. When Cromwell garrisoned the castle, he built a massive extension to accommodate his men. That area is now the library, and it is in this space that the ghost of a man often appears. The apparition has been seen sitting in a chair next to the fireplace, but vanishes when approached. Could the Duke be warming his spirit by the hearth, still chafing over his untimely death?

The other ghost known to haunt the castle is a female spirit familiarly called the Gray Lady. It is commonly reported that this apparition is thought to be the ghost of one of three women who starved to death in the dungeons where they were placed because they had the plague. Those reports are false, according to a ghost-hunting group that has spent time investigating the spirits at Brodick Castle. David Smith of Scottish Paranormal Investigations (SPI) says they have spoken with family members as well as conducted overnight vigils, and the information given to them is quite different. According to Lady Jean, the youngest daughter of the Duchess and Duke of Montrose and the last of the lineage to live at Brodick, the Gray Lady is the spirit of a servant girl who lived in the 17th century. What's more, the servant also is connected to Cromwell's forces because she had an intimate relationship with the captain of the guard. When she became pregnant, she was quickly dismissed from her duties at the castle and her family disowned her. The devastated woman committed suicide by throwing herself into the sea near the entrance to the castle gates. Her spirit moved back into the halls that she used to silently walk as a servant, overseeing the work of those now employed to keep the floors and furniture spic and span. She was spotted standing over people as they scrubbed the floors, though the person doing the work did not notice her; it was a third party who caught the ghost supervising. It looked as though she was also talking to the worker, perhaps offering otherworldly advice or admonition for substandard scrubbing. Witnesses claim to have seen the Gray Lady outside the Servants' Hall, now the tearoom, and on the stairs that once were the servants' entrance to the castle. Lady Jean told SPI there were several incidents after they hired a clairvoyant housekeeper, including sightings in the Round Room and on the castle grounds.

A team of researchers and psychics from SPI experienced several strange occurrences during two different overnight

*A team of researchers and psychics from Scottish Paranormal
Investigations set up for their overnight investigation.*

investigations at the castle. David Smith says that most recently,
while they were busy in the servants' quarters setting up
remote cameras and testing to see if they had them properly
positioned, he noticed out of the corner of his eye one of the
old wrought iron lights moving. He looked and sure enough
it was swaying. "It was in a full swing, not like it had been
disturbed by a breeze," he explained. He grabbed his digital
camera and caught the movement to show property manager
Bill Cowell. They tried to determine if there might be *any*
possible explanation for the swinging light, but there were no
drafts and no open doors, nothing to account for the sub-
stantial amount of sway. While on location in July 2003, the
team saw dark shadows, sensed they were being watched,
photographed a number of orbs, and during a séance picked

up on several other spirits from various times in the castle's history. One of the psychics tuned into the unusual presence of a man saying someone was in trouble for swimming at the outdoor pool. When they later asked the property manager about a road hazard sign they had seen on the way from the castle, he told them it marked a condemned swimming hole that had been shut down many years ago. Is it possible someone drowned there and the submerged spirit still tries to warn people of the danger?

The other strange sightings may be merely legend, but it is said that a white stag appears on the castle grounds or near to the castle when one of the Chiefs of the Hamilton clan dies or is near death. Since there hasn't been a death or a sighting in a while, this one is harder to prove. The existence of white stags is real, although seeing them is quite rare.

Brodick Castle may be better known in some circles for its famous collection of rhododendrons than its crew of phantoms, but there is still quite a bit of paranormal weirdness within its walls. The ferry ride alone—with its stunning views of Goatfell Mountain—makes it worth the trip to check out the ghosts for yourself.

# Tragedy in Chillingham
## NORTHUMBERLAND, ENGLAND

Strategically placed on the northeastern border between England and Scotland, Chillingham Castle occupies a key place in the country's history books as a site of bloody sieges and horrible tortures in its dungeons. From its earliest days as a 12th-century stronghold through to becoming a 14th-century castle fortress and right up to present day, the Grey family and their ancestors have lived in the sprawling stone castle. Many have died to protect the land on which this huge mansion sits. They fought in every war from Agincourt to World War II, and on many occasions Chillingham was taken captive and the Greys grappled to win the castle back. It is now home to Sir Humphrey and the Honorable Lady Wakefield. Oh yes, and at least half a dozen ghosts. This is an historic and very haunted castle.

The "Blue Boy" and Lady Mary Berkeley are the most famous of Chillingham's ghosts. Those living at the castle now accept them as part of an "extended family" because they have been part of the castle's history for so long. They even dedicate several pages to the many ghosts on the castle's Internet site, so those who want to book a banquet or wedding can become well acquainted with the otherworldly souls that may join the party. Sir Humphrey, a gracious man with whom I had a lovely conversation about Chillingham's ghosts, says he feels quite protected by the spirits within his home. "At first the dark seemed quite frightening," he says of the days 20 years ago when he first lived in Chillingham. "Now I find it quite comforting and protective." His initial fears prompted him to seek out a local priest well versed in dealing with spirits to have him perform an exorcism. "When he first came, the priest said to me, 'Don't bother, they are far too strong.' I had him come back a second time some months later and the priest said there was no need to do an exorcism because he said, 'the spirits support you now.'" Since then, Sir Humphrey says he is sure the ghosts "protect me like mad." As an example, he recalled working on renovations and was putting in windows two stories up when he lost his balance and fell. Amazingly, he landed on a pile of straw that had not seemed close enough to break his fall.

Most guests won't have an opportunity to see the Blue Boy because he haunted a room that is no longer open to the public. His agonizing cries of pain, heard when the clock tower struck midnight, suggested that a horrible death befell the young lad. Who is he? How did he die? No one seems to know. But it would seem his spirit, though it didn't immediately pass on to the next plane, did not lurk about only to cause others anguish. The noises emanated from the "Pink Room" at a point in the wall next to a passage cut through to the adjoining tower. As the sound of the boy's cries faded, witnesses claimed to then see a bright light shine by the four-poster bed. The boy walked within the circle of light, a gentle figure wearing blue clothes from the Restoration period (1660s). As it turns out, the sound of the boy's blood-curdling cries came from the same place in the wall where the skeleton of a small child and remnants of a blue outfit were found during renovations in the 1920s. Could it be that the boy was buried alive? A chilling discovery, doubly so because the boy's bones were found alongside the skeleton of a man found in the place where there is now a fireplace. Both bodies were near a trap door that opened to stone arches of vaults beneath. Once the remains were properly buried in a local churchyard, the tales of seeing the Blue Boy stopped. However, strange blue flashes of light occasionally awaken people sleeping in the room. At first it was thought that there might be some sort of short in the wires, but there is no electrical wiring anywhere near where the blue flashes take place.

The tragedy of Lady Mary Berkeley, abandoned by her husband, seems to be the best-documented tale in its direct connection to former inhabitants of Chillingham. Listed as a direct descendant of King Henry VIII, Lady Mary had a lineage that could not escape marital strife. Her philandering spouse, Ford, Lord Grey of Wark and Chillingham and Earl of Tankerville, ran off with Lady Henrietta, Mary's sister. This event occurred during the reign of King Charles II and caused a huge scandal in the upper class, ending in a lawsuit before the notorious Judge Jeffries (see the story of Plas Teg). When Lord Grey and his supporters were brought to trial in November 1682, his mistress and a number of staunch Whigs boldly accompanied him into court. Judge Jeffries found the unfaithful husband guilty, but as his friends banded together to resist, something very like a riot ensued. Two years after the trial, the famous *Love Letters between a Nobleman and his Sister* was published—a romantic collection of prose that supposedly passed between the two lovers, though many are sure author Aphra Behn (the first Englishwoman to earn a living by writing) wrote the lyrical words. Lord Grey died June 25, 1701. Henrietta died nine years later. But it was poor Lady Mary, left alone with a baby daughter, who lived out the rest of her years alone in the huge, empty castle. Betrayed, heartbroken, she died May 19, 1719. Perhaps it was her frustration and pent-up anger that kept her tied to this mortal coil; her dress has been heard rustling briskly along the corridors and up the stairs and those who hear her pass have also said they felt a bone-chilling cold pass through them. There have also been less likely reports of seeing her spirit "escape" from her portrait, which was hung in the nursery. Nannies and children say they saw Lady Mary step out of the frame, like something out of *Mary Poppins*, and wander off in search of her wayward husband. Sir Humphrey says the portrait is no longer in the castle—it went to the Christie's auction house. He actually tried to get it back but it had already been sold. "I don't think she wanted to come back," he says, adding that may be a sign that Lady Mary's spirit is moving on.

The other ghosts haunt the pantry, a former bedchamber and the library. In the library, people often claim to hear the voices of two men talking. No actual dialogue can be heard, just the distinct mumble of male voices. The ghost of a woman who may have died by poisoning and whose spirit still thirsts for a drink of water haunts what is known as the "inner pantry." That's the room where the good silver used to be locked up. For good measure, a footman was locked in with the utensils at night to make sure they weren't stolen. One evening a frail, pale woman in white appeared and asked the startled footman for a glass of water. He went to get it for her, thinking a visitor had lost her way, but he suddenly remembered the room was locked. When he turned to ask the woman where she was from, the footman found himself alone. The figure in white had vanished. A psychic with no prior knowledge of the castle's spirits named this ghost in a tour of the rooms, and specifically mentioned the need for water because it was a woman who had died by poison many centuries ago.

The other ghost cited by Chillingham's owners seems to occupy a bedroom in which a former chef committed suicide. After a woman who had been given the room was found sleeping on a sofa in the dining hall, terrified and unwilling to return to her quarters, the owners decided to close it up and no longer use it.

The "nanny" ghost is an unusual member of the castle's spectral family. Sir Humphrey says certain rooms are haunted by a spirit that makes the beds and tickles people's toes. Guests who rent these rooms claim to also hear children laughing and playing. "The origin of that one is unknown," says Sir Humphrey.

During restoration to the King James chamber, a painter was hired to work on the ceiling. As he stood on scaffolding to reach the room's upper limit, a man came along wearing a 16th-century smock. The fellow shook his head in disapproval though he didn't say anything. The painter continued his work, thinking someone was playing a joke on him. He was stunned to see the man in period clothes return when the work was finished, only this time the mysterious man smiled at the painter, pleased it would seem with the final results.

As a way of covering the astronomical costs of keeping up a castle, tourists have been invited to visit Chillingham for the last 20 years or so. The ghosts seem to like the extra company. "They enjoy the tourists coming around," Sir Humphrey told me, "and perform for them admirably." Guest records in the last six months include several accounts in a castle journal of people seeing dark figures in the dungeons, the figure of a young child, and hearing the voice of a child trapped behind a wall. The ghosts also perform on cue, as it were, when television cameras arrive to shoot video for the recent spate of "reality" programs that deal with the paranormal. It started with a Japanese television crew back in 1998 that was truly terrified by the time they left, and their program sent ghost hunters to the castle in droves. Sir Humphrey says times were tough back then and they were desperately in need of income—he feels the ghosts did their part to help out. Since then, several shows have captured some of the strange happenings on tape. "We had another show called 'The Big Breakfast' (on BBC) and we took the crew into the torture chamber. Almost immediately one of the dogs' hackles went up and then one of the torture machines started moving on its own," recalls Sir Humphrey.

Other ghost stories connected to the castle are of a distinctly personal nature. In the memoirs of Lady Leonora Tankerville, wife of Lord George Bennet, she recounts several supernatural incidents that occurred during her residence at Chillingham in the 1920s. "The first time I ever saw Chillingham was in the company of a so-called ghost," she wrote. On her first visit to the castle, she tells of how she did not know her way about and was met by a young man who introduced himself as her future husband's brother. "I have come to walk with you until George is ready," he told her. When Lord Bennet arrived the young man disappeared, and not in the "make oneself scarce" way. He simply vanished. It turns out he had died two years earlier, but could not bring himself to cross over until his brother found someone with whom he could settle down. Lady Leonora also witnessed the ghostly apparition of a sick friend who came to her one evening as she prepared for bed. She told her husband of the visit and that she felt it was a good-bye; they found out the next day that the man had died at the same time as his appearance in Leonora's dressing room.

Chillingham is a stunning castle, surrounded by the beauty of Northumberland and the wealth of the Earls Grey—yes, those of the tea renown—and it is definitely open to the public. Even if you don't encounter one of the more famous ghosts, you may well bump into one of the many dozens of spirits said to float through the castle courtyard. There are, after all, 800 years of battles, revelry, carousing, cheating, births, deaths and all the lives in between from which to fill a castle's keep.

# The Diva Lives On
## BRECON BEACONS NATIONAL PARK, WALES

In Wales, like the rest of the island of which it is part, there are more ghosts, as my grandmother used to say, than you can shake a stick at. One of the best places to find them in abundance is within the thick stone walls of old castles where the ambiance combines with links to the past to weave together an aura of eeriness. Craig Y Nos Castle is no exception. Ask any local ghost hunter and he or she will likely have been on a visit or overnight vigil to the Gothic structure in search of ghosts or to soak up the spectral atmosphere. The ghosts of an opera diva who was embalmed in its cellar and patients who died while being nursed for tuberculosis are among the many spirits said to haunt the castle's various rooms.

To find Craig Y Nos Castle, head for the beautiful Brecon Beacons National Park in the Upper Swansea Valley in South Wales. It is now a hotel, but at the turn of the 20th century it belonged to world-famous opera singer Adelina Patti, one of the highest paid sopranos to grace a stage. She bought the massive gray stone manor from the Powell family; it was Captain Rice Powell who had built the castle in 1843 using the money he made from mining in India. In 1919, at age 76, Adelina fell down a staircase and her injuries left her bedridden. She soon developed pneumonia and died. Most of the paranormal activity in the castle is attributed to the singing star or her two husbands, the Marquis of Caux and Ernesto Nicolini.

The castle's cellar provides particularly creepy energy: that is where Adelina's body was embalmed. In the "Slab Room"—the name alone is horrible enough—the singer's coffin was sealed with hot lead. During one ghost watch, the eight pins in a woman's long, tightly bound hair suddenly fell to the floor, pulled out by an unseen hand. The coiled hair unraveled, much to the woman's surprise. She was alone and could not explain how the pins all came loose at the same time. Opera sopranos are stereotyped as jealous, catty women—could it be that in death Adelina couldn't help herself from picking on another woman?

Petty, perhaps. Pious, most definitely. Adelina had her own chapel—now a hotel bridal suite—and would say prayers daily with a priest. When the current owners took over the castle, the chapel and adjoining vestry were a terrible mess with holes in the ceiling. The vestry had been sealed up—it looks like during the hospital days someone tried to make it a bathroom but gave up—and when it was opened, a bible was found on a window ledge. Over a few months, workers and staff reported that the bible constantly moved about as if Adelina's priest still carried it on his daily visits to her while she prayed.

In the castle's jazz bar, appropriately named the Patti Bar, the former singer apparently likes to chat up the musicians. According to the people running the hotel, a drummer named Dave Cottle sat waiting in a corner for two of his fellow musicians and struck up a conversation with a woman in black sitting by the fireplace. She asked if he sang and Cottle replied that he only played instruments. The woman seemed dismayed. "So you don't sing then," she replied. "It's a shame." When Cottle's band mates arrived, they surprised him by asking who he was talking to. "The lady in the corner," he told them as if they were pulling his leg. They told him there was no one there that they could see. Dave Cottle went white as he suddenly realized he spent the last several minutes talking to a ghost. Other reports say that the sound of the song "Home Sweet Home" is a surefire way to bring Adelina's ghost into the room. During World War II, two young nurses heard a female voice singing scales in the corridors outside their room. Terrified, they moved to sleep in a different room that night. It was said that Adelina used to practice her scales every day until the day she died. Could it be she was warming up for an angelic chorus?

One of the additions built by Adelina was a theater in which she sang to many a bejeweled audience, royalty and dignitaries rubbing shoulders for a chance to hear her golden-throated tones. It should come as no surprise that this is one of her favorite haunts. A lady pianist claimed that one night as she was performing in the theater she felt a strange presence envelop her. Surrounded by this energy, she began playing a piece of music that was unknown to her, without making a single mistake. The owner of the castle, a man named Martin, did not believe in all the ghost stories when he took possession of Craig Y Nos; one night on the Patti Theatre stage in 2001 changed all that. He planned to deliver a conference speech on Halloween and decided to lock himself into the theater one evening to practice after everyone had gone home for the day. As he stood on stage, he saw one of the doors that had been closed swing open. He was quite sure he had pulled all the doors firmly shut, and they all had solid steel bolts that snap in place. So Martin simply assumed someone else was working late and continued slogging through

*Adelina Patti, a diva even in death, still vies for attention in the Craig Y Nos Castle.*

his speech. It was nearing midnight when he wrapped up and when he walked over to the doors, he found them *all* wide open. He looked about but the castle was empty—he was the only person in the building. Martin knew he had carefully bolted the doors closed from the inside, making sure the bolts were locked both top and bottom. There was no explanation for the doors being open. Martin, in that moment, realized he had been introduced to Madame Patti.

Adelina is a prominent phantom, a diva even in death; however, she is by no means the only castle ghost. The Nicolini Bar, named after Adelina's second husband, is haunted by his ghost. It used to be Ernesto Nicolini's library. Employees and guests claim to have heard a man shouting out orders. On the staircase, a photograph taken during a May 2004 investigation by the Ghost Research Foundation International (GRFI) seems to be proof positive of a male spirit that haunts the building. While touring the rooms, a psychic with the team felt a distinct presence on the stairs and several photographs were taken in the area. Though nothing was visible to the assembled group, when the pictures were downloaded to a laptop, the clear image of a man standing on the staircase emerged. GRFI president Paul Howse said the way the picture was taken ruled out the possibility that it was just a shadow of someone in the room. In an interview for the icWales Network Paul said, "It was totally dark at the time and we were using infrared night-vision photography to capture images in zero light conditions. This combined with the fact that the 'figure' was in the precise position that Norie [the psychic] had described makes this an amazing result." Since then, other guests claim to have captured the ghost image on video.

Other ghosts are connected to the time when the castle housed tuberculosis patients. The wraith-like apparitions of patients have been seen wandering around the building, particularly in the Billiard and Music Rooms. In the Conservatory, which was a children's ward, the tragic cries of little children and babies can be heard wailing for comfort. Even the Auditorium orchestra pit, of all places, is said to be haunted by children. A ghost watch team that slept in this area beneath the stage heard children giggling and laughing and what sounded like a ball being bounced. A separate group—with no knowledge of the ghost investigation—was housed in the cellar bedrooms on New Year's Eve 2003 and reported hearing a ball bounce. It turns out this space was a play area during the castle's hospital period.

Dozens of paranormal investigations—too many to include here—have been carried out at Craig Y Nos, each one finding something worth reporting. The reports contain many similarities, and lots of new things like odd sounds and creaks that may be significant or may just be a bit of susceptibility to the castle's spooky atmosphere. Really though, does it matter? When there are so many documented experiences, why quibble over one or two moans and groans?

# Dragsholm Slot
## HØRVE, ZEALAND ISLAND, DENMARK

An insane baron, a noble maiden imprisoned for her affair with a commoner and a grateful servant—it sounds like the cast of a Shakespearean plot but instead makes up the trio of ghosts in Denmark's Dragsholm Slot. A Gray Lady, a White Lady and the ghost of the Earl of Bothwell love to tease the staff, play games with the lights and occasionally show off for the guests. "It's not dangerous, but it can be a little spooky," is how tour guide Kirsten Rasmussen summed up her three and a half years at the castle.

Kirsten retired a few years ago, then picked up work at Dragsholm Slot (*slot* means castle in Danish) taking guests around to the church, dungeons and castle theater to tell them about both the history and the hauntings. The history doesn't take that long to tell; the ghostly goings-on could fill several pages. (Kirsten told me she has at least a dozen pages written of things that she has witnessed in her short time there.) The Bishop of Roskilde built the castle at the beginning of the 13th century. It became a royal castle after the Dano-Swedish war in the middle of the 17th century. The Adeler family took it over in 1694 and it remained in their possession for nearly two and a half centuries, during which time the status of the estate was changed to *lensbaroni* or barony from the Crown. The Bøttger family bought the property by Nekselø Bugt (bay), with its moat and ancient rhododendron plantation, from the state in 1937 and converted the castle into a hotel. Soon after the guests began arriving, the Bøttgers learned they had ghosts, because the ghosts were not all that

*Dragsholm Slot is a paranormal paradise with three main ghosts known to roam its halls.*

happy with the disruption of their quiet, and hitherto almost sole domain. Even now, they act up whenever there is a lot of noise or some sort of major renovation. Kirsten recalls seeing the cook coming rushing out of the kitchen one day during a time of massive renovations in that area. There had been hammering all day and apparently the spirits were distressed. "The cook came out and said he didn't want to be in there. It was too spooky. The oven doors and the cabinet doors were all opening and shutting by themselves. The mixer the cook had been using went crazy, spraying batter all over the walls. He had been a cook for 10 years and never saw anything like it," says Kirsten. "They hated the noise."

On another occasion, it was the guests who caused the disturbance. A large party of heavy drinkers became very unruly when it came time to take the tour. Kirsten took them into the church, but the alcohol had numbed their senses. "One of the girls was very noisy and swore. It was very stupid. I asked her to keep her voice down or leave," recalls Kirsten. When the group left the church for the Great Hall, suddenly the light went out. Kirsten checked, and somehow the dimmer had been turned down. "The group got a little quiet, for a moment." She continued with the tour, taking them to another part of the house where there were bones found in the wall. The noisy party still babbled as Kirsten tried in vain to tell the story of the White Lady. Suddenly *all* the lights went out. "It was completely dark, and they got very scared," says Kirsten. "I was annoyed because it wasn't funny. None of the staff would do something like this because it isn't amusing. I tried to find the light on the wall, groping around and eventually found it but it wouldn't go on. Finally I said under my breath, 'Come on, turn it on!' and it went on." A week later some clairvoyants came to castle, and Kirsten asked them about the incident. She says they surprised her by saying there was another spirit in the church, a very old preacher from the late 1700s who hates people and really hates people coming into his church. "They told me he surely shut off the light because he didn't want you and those drunken people to be there."

There are a lot of ghosts in the castle, but many are not that interesting, according to Kirsten. The three main ones tend to be publicized: the Gray Lady, the White Lady and the Earl. The Gray Lady is seen infrequently; she is said to be a former housekeeper who lived at the castle. Shortly before her death in the mid-1600s she suffered from a serious toothache which caused her horrendous pain. She was cured and the story goes that she haunts the halls making sure everything is in order as a token of her eternal gratitude for being released from the excruciating pain. The White Lady is said to be the daughter of one of the many owners of the castle. She fell in love with commoner who worked in the castle and they began a love affair. They kept their relationship secret for some time, but the girl's father eventually found out. Furious that his daughter should betray him with a commoner, he ordered the servants of the castle to imprison his daughter inside a thick wall of the castle. It is said that because of the tragic event, she returns to the castle most nights and walks around the corridors. Until the 1930s the story was mainly legend, but during renovations to install new toilets, workers tore down an old wall and found a small hole in the crumbling mortar. Behind it was a skeleton wrapped in a white dress.

The castle dungeon held many prisoners, but none so famous as James Hepburn, 4th Earl of Bothwell (sometimes referred to as the Forgotten Scot). The Scottish nobleman led a turbulent life and ended up being run out of the country after he divorced his wife and married Mary, Queen of Scots. He was captured in Denmark in 1567 fleeing from his own countrymen and was imprisoned at Dragsholm Slot. Chained to a wall in the dungeon for about five years, he paced until he wore a crescent-shaped ditch into the stone. He also went mad and died in 1578 in the cellar. The Earl now lies at rest in Fårevejle Church, about three miles from the castle; Lord Bothwell's ghost, however, is said to come riding in the courtyard of the castle with his horse carriage. Some guests have heard horses hooves scramble in the courtyard as if someone was riding out there, but it is vacant when they look. Why Bothwell would remain at the place that resulted in his death is difficult to fathom—could it be that his insanity caused his spirit to be locked on this plane, unaware that he is dead and able to move on?

The number of stories told by guests and employees should be enough to convince most people that the castle is a paranormal paradise. Kirsten says they also regularly receive photographs from guests asking for an explanation to the white mist or bluish translucent figure captured on film. "We usually just say that 'we think it is whatever you think it is.'" But a group of American parapsychologists recently visited the castle with special equipment to gather measurable data—tangible proof of the spirits' existence. Andrew Nichols spent three days taking instrument readings at the various sites where people claimed to experience paranormal phenomena, and in some areas he found extreme levels of electricity and radioactivity. Nichols documented high levels of electromagnetic field (EMF) in the Gray Lady's room where researchers in 1996 had previously found an EMF anomaly. In the fourth-floor theater, he recorded a sudden drop in temperature and reported seeing a person in light-colored flowing clothes move out of the corner of his left eye. The only other people in the castle at the time were three maids working in the kitchen and dining room on the first floor. In an article about his experience written for the *Journal of Parapsychology* in 1999, Nichols wrote, "In the past, scientists have dismissed haunting experiences as psychological fantasies with no basis in the real world. Investigations by the authors and others suggest that the phenomena are real, and that they may have a physical source."

Kirsten Rasmussen doesn't question the presence of the ghosts. She knows they exist. "Now and then they help me. For instance if I have an audience of elderly men, they think I'm a crazy woman," she laughs. "I don't care, but one day I was facing two or three of these skeptical men and suddenly one of their cell phones rang." She watched in amusement as the group berated the man, who claimed he was sure he had shut it off. "Two minutes later another rang, and he said 'I swear I shut mine off,' but then it wouldn't turn off and he had to leave the room." Kirsten watched as the non-believers suddenly changed their tune.

On other occasions, the ghosts aren't quite so obliging. One of the waitresses working in the Great Hall had lit all the candles and was putting out the cups and saucers for coffee when all of a sudden the candles were somehow extinguished. All at once. No huge breeze blew through. Irritated because of the time it takes to relight them all, the woman hurried to get them all burning again and then went down to the restaurant to get the coffee. When she returned, the gray figure of a very tall woman stood before her. The waitress exclaimed out loud, and the apparition quickly moved off to a chair in the corner that she is known to occupy, but not before making all the candles go out again. Kirsten Rasmussen experienced much the same thing while working in the hall, watching candles go out before her eyes right after she had lit them.

Fjords and phantoms could be the ideal match—it seems worth a trip to the town of Hørve to find out. As Kirsten Rasmussen puts it, "It's a very exciting place."

# Great Glamis!
## FORFAR, TAYSIDE, SCOTLAND

The raven himself is hoarse
That croaks the fatal entrance of Duncan
Under my battlements. Come, you spirits
That tend on mortal thoughts, unsex me here,
And fill me from the crown to the toe top-full
Of direst cruelty!
Great Glamis! Worthy Cawdor!
Greater than both, by the all-hail hereafter!
Thy letters have transported me beyond
This ignorant present, and I feel now
The future in an instant.
                    —Lady MacBeth, *MacBeth*, Act I, Scene V

The huge medieval stronghold of Glamis Castle, near Forfar, Scotland, would impress any passerby…and perhaps send a chill up their spine. Who can forget Lady MacBeth's murderous incantation in plotting the murder of King Duncan so that her husband might rise from his "lowly" station as Thane of Glamis? That was Shakespeare's fantasy, but the massive 14th-century castle houses some very real ghosts, and their stories keep the tourists coming and the locals on their toes. There's a monster, a vampire and a veritable who's who of ghouls to ensure Glamis Castle maintains its status as the most haunted castle in the United Kingdom.

As Scotland's oldest inhabited castle, Glamis is believed to be haunted by more than two dozen spirits. Some of the ghosts have absolutely no connection to its history. The castle in northeast Scotland has been the ancestral home of the Earls of Strathmore and Kinghorne since 1372 when Sir John Lyon of Forteviot became Thane of Glamis and was given the castle by King Robert II of Scotland. Four years later, it entered the royal real estate holdings when Sir John married Princess Joanna, the King's daughter. Since then, Glamis Castle has housed many members of the British and Scottish royal families. It was the childhood home of Queen Elizabeth the Queen Mother, and the birthplace of Princess Margaret. Mystery and melancholy billow around the vast, ancient walls, even when surrounded by summer's blooms. The entire structure seems slightly askew as if perched between two worlds. It is often said that, strangely enough, the number of windows as seen from within and then counted again from outside never add up.

Of all the ghosts within Glamis Castle, two stand out as the perennial favorites, having been seen over the years by various witnesses who report roughly the same details each time. The spirit of the profligate 4th Earl of Strathmore, christened Alexander but known generally as "Earl Beardie," frequently stomps about the castle, doomed to spend eternity within its walls after staking his soul in a game with the devil. As the tale goes, Earl Beardie came by his hard-drinking, gambling ways naturally—his family had already lost the family fortune in the mid-17th century. Patrick Lyons inherited the disintegrating manor and rebuilt the family coffers (for which he was made 1st Earl of Strathmore), but in the early 18th century Earl Beardie reintroduced bad habits back into castle life. There are a couple of versions to this legend, but the bottom line is that one night Earl Beardie was so determined to play cards he announced he would happily ante up with the devil if no one else would oblige him. The devil naturally took him up on his invitation, appearing as a tall, dark man wearing a black coat and hat. It seems obvious but the devil won every hand, taking not only Earl Beardie's money, but also his soul with him when he vanished. Five years later, Earl Beardie died. His terrible penance became clear soon after his death as he was heard stamping his feet and cursing in a rage in a room high up in the uninhabited West Tower. Castle servants swear they have heard the rattle of dice at night and the sounds of an angry man coming from the locked, empty room. Still others claim to have seen his ghost roaming in other parts of the castle. Lord Halifax apparently saw Earl Beardie's ghost when he spent a night at Glamis Castle. Other guests at the castle claim to have awakened at 4 AM to see his ghost leaning over them, peering at them. On stormy nights, he has been seen out on the roof swearing and stamping about at a spot known now as "Mad Earl's Walk"—perhaps hoping to find the devil and try his luck at winning his soul back?

The second well-known ghost is the wraith of the tormented Janet Douglas, who was burned at the stake in the 16th century for allegedly attempting to kill King James V. Janet was already on shaky ground after her husband, the 6th Lord of Glamis, keeled over dead one morning shortly after eating breakfast. Fingers pointed at Janet, though no proof condemned her of the deed. Six years later, she was accused of attempting to poison the king. Some believe King James used her as a scapegoat in a feud with her brother; regardless, she was charged with being a witch and in 1537 she died on a pyre at Castle Hill, Edinburgh. She now haunts the clock tower, appearing swathed in flames or casting a reddish glow.

*Many believe that Glamis Castle has hidden chambers or passageways deep within the castle.*

A figure known as the Gray Lady has made several appearances in the chapel dedicated to Saint Michael. This pious phantom generally kneels in one of the pews or is seen walking into the chapel. No one knows who she is or why she haunts the chapel. Lady Granville, the sister to the Queen Mother, witnessed the Gray Lady at length and was able to describe in some detail what she wore. Lady Granville knew she was seeing a ghost when she saw a beam of sunlight streaming through a chapel window shine right *through* the praying figure. This ghost is one of the few that are making current appearances. I contacted some local ghost tour operators in search of new, up-to-date stories of any of the ghosts to include in this book and for the most part was told they haven't heard of any recent sightings. But I came across a report on a BBC web site from a Canadian traveler who toured Glamis Castle when he was 18. Ken reported that his tour group was leaving and he lingered for a moment to look at the chapel paintings. "When I looked up, the tour group had left. I immediately went after them and just as I was about to leave the chapel, I turned to have one last look. In the last pew, there was a nun kneeling in prayer," wrote Ken. "She had a gray habit and she raised her head and looked at me. She had an expression of extreme sadness. Her face was gray like her habit and I immediately knew that I was seeing something that was not there just 30 seconds before, as I had been in that last pew looking at the paneled paintings." Until that moment, Ken says he was unaware of Glamis' ghosts. "I had no knowledge of ghosts in this castle beforehand. It happened. I accepted that and to this day, if I close my eyes, I can see her clearly in my mind. The encounter was virtually burned into my memory."

There are so many other ghosts it is hard to know where to begin. There's the specter of a little child known as the Black Boy. He sits on a stone seat at the door to the Queen Mum's sitting room. Legend has it that he was a servant badly treated—some reports suggest he may have been left out in the cold and died of exposure. His ghost may have tried to even the score because people who slept in the room complained that they could feel something tug at their blankets, trying to pull them off the bed during the night. The strange activity ceased after the room was converted to a bathroom. The ghost of a former butler haunts the unused Hangman's Chamber where the man took his own life. The figure of a "huge old man" frightened the daughter of a former Lord Castleton while she visited; she awoke to see the ghost sitting in front of the fire and when he turned to look at her, she saw the face was "that of a dead man." A thin yet elusive ghost seen loping up the castle drive on moonlit nights earned the nickname "Jack the Runner." Glamis' vampire is more the stuff of local legend, but some swear the creature exists, locked within the walls of the castle. It is said that a woman servant was caught sucking the blood of her victim and she was somehow overpowered and entombed alive within a secret chamber in the thick, stone walls where she waits even now to be released.

A tongueless woman (some reports also have her as having no hands as well) runs across the grounds at night, gesturing at her bloody maw. The ghost of another woman with large, mournful eyes has been seen pressing her face against a window as if imprisoned. One visitor who happened to be up late one night apparently saw the pale-faced woman gazing helplessly from the window. She suddenly vanished, dragged away by an unseen person with inordinate strength. The guest waited to see if she would reappear, and was horrified by the sound of violent screams tearing through the castle walls.

The Monster of Glamis, though not a ghost per se, is worth telling because the castle bears the karmic scars of this unpleasant story. At the turn of the 19th century, the 11th Earl of Strathmore had a first-born son who more resembled a beast than a boy. Described as being egg-shaped with a huge, hairy body, no neck and tiny arms and legs, this deformed creature's birthright entitled him to inherit the Strathmore estate. His family, however, could not bear to look on the hideous Monster of Glamis, and they apparently hid him away in a secret chamber fully expecting him to die an early death because of his condition. The Monster surprised everyone and thrived. In fact, he lived for over 100 years, locked away inside the castle, and is believed to have died in 1921.

Rather than admit his existence and turn over the estate, the family moved to shroud the Monster by allowing only four people to know he lived: the Earl, his second son, the family lawyer and the factor of the estate. The estate passed—unlawfully—into the hands of the Monster's younger brother. Years passed and the Monster of Glamis stayed hidden in his castle prison. As each successive heir reached the age of 21, he was told the secret and taken to see the creature who was the true heir. The revelation naturally shocked each of the earls, and rumor has it the sight of the dwarf permanently changed each man, leaving them sadder and more moody.

None of the women was ever told of the grim secret, though one Lady Strathmore heard the rumors and (according to a Scottish tour operator named Sandy) asked the estate factor at the time, a Mr. Ralston, if there was any truth to them. He reportedly denied the story, but went on to tell the woman "it is fortunate you do not know the truth for if you did you would never be happy." This same man refused to sleep in the castle, to the point where even a sudden snowstorm would not delay his departure. He demanded that a pathway be shoveled for him all the way from the castle to his home a mile away. The unfortunate creature born to privilege and treated as inhuman is not to be found in any official records; however, there is a portrait hanging within the castle that depicts one of the earls surrounded by two sons—and a hideously deformed dwarf.

Though the Monster's life remains a mystery, there are documents to suggest the secret chamber does exist. It's just hidden deep within the castle. And going back to that note about the castle having more windows outside than inside—a group of visiting schoolchildren was determined to find the secret chamber. While Lord Strathmore was out hunting, the children ran throughout the castle hanging sheets and towels out of every window. When they went outside, to their utter amazement they counted not one but seven unaccounted windows. There is also a newspaper report that dates back to 1880 that tells of a stonemason who discovered more than he should have. He apparently knocked a hole in one of the castle walls to reveal a passageway that led to a hidden, locked room. The man received a large sum of money under the condition that he leave the country and keep his mouth shut.

Where does that leave the ghosts of Glamis Castle? Sandy Stevenson, a tour operator who visits the castle regularly, tells me there are no new sightings. But with this long list of creepy critters and the castle's haunted history, is there any doubt that one of the shadows lurking in the many hallways and corners is not actually a ghost in waiting?

# Ruthin Castle
## Denbighshire, Wales

The romantic Ruthin Castle of North Wales has a wonderful web site that declares the 13th-century estate is "truly individual…truly magical…" It left out truly haunted. Mind you, the castle owners cannot be faulted, as this story came to me from one woman who is a direct descendant of the clans that clashed and died there hundreds of years ago. Stacy Jones' experience left her shaken and sure that her bloodline still has enemies in the spirits that haunt Ruthin Castle's extensive grounds.

The name Ruthin comes from the Welsh words for red (*rhudd*) and fort (*din*). This is where the history is important in the context of Stacy's story. She sent me an excerpt from a book called *History of the Gwydir Family and Memoirs* by Sir John Wynn. The excerpt is about the forest near Ruthin and it reminded Stacy of her experience. She also noted that the author, Sir John Wynn, as well as John ap Maredudd and his son Morus are her ancestors. The excerpt is as follows:

John ap Maredudd had 5 sons: Morus, Gruffudd, Robert, Owain, and Ieuan. Robert, in his father's time, was slain without issue near Ruthin. The Thelwalls of Ruthin, being ancient gentlemen of that country, who came into that country with the Lord Grey, to whom King Edward the first bestowed the country of Dyffryn Clwyd, being at contention with a sect or kindred of that country called the family of Gruffudd Goch. These, being more in number than the Thelwalls, drove the Thelwalls to take the castle of Ruthin for their defence where they besieged them until the siege was raised by John ap Maredudd's sons and kindred to whom the Thelwalls sent for aid. In that exploit, Robert, the son of John ap Maredudd, was slain with an arrow in a wood within view of the castle of Ruthin called Coed Marchan, in revenge whereof many of the other side were slain both at that time and after.

Stacy had no knowledge of any of this family bloodshed or ties to Ruthin prior to a holiday she took in July 1995. At the time, she was working at a travel agency. She says that because her agency sold a massive number of tickets for one airline carrier, that company gave all the agents in the office a free business-class ticket to anywhere in the world, and a half-price ticket for a second person. Stacy used her tickets to take her mother on a trip to the UK, traveling to Ireland, England, Wales and Scotland. Their time at Ruthin Castle would end up being one of the most significant and supernatural moments of the entire tour.

Right from the get-go Wales put Stacy at ease in a way she had never expected. "How else do I explain the fact that as soon as I stepped in Wales, I felt like I was just coming home from a long trip? Like that's where I really belonged? That's not just an interest in something. It's more of an inside or instinctive feeling. And I'm also Irish, so why didn't I feel that way in Ireland? These are questions I ask myself all the time."

Stacy and her mother arrived in Denbighshire on a Sunday. "Strangely enough, we had the hotel to ourselves," she told me. "The only other people we saw other than a few staff members were in the morning when we went to breakfast. There were two other people eating, and that's it." They enjoyed Ruthin's warm and welcoming atmosphere. There was certainly no sense of any hostile ghosts. Ironically, Stacy really felt quite at ease, connecting to the space as if it were her home. "Our room even reminded me of my great-grandmother's room back home."

Outside Ruthin Castle, the mood shifted. Stacy tuned in to a much more sinister feeling. "There was dead silence, except for the sounds of peacocks roaming around the castle, which sounded eerie." In spite of the ominous overtones, Stacy and her mom ventured out for a tour of the area. While they strolled around the grounds, they saw in the distance a stone circle with a type of altar in the middle. Getting to the shrine meant walking through a small thicket of trees near the castle. It may have been small, but it packed a supernatural wallop. "While walking through, I all of a sudden got a very creepy feeling, like someone didn't want me there, or like hatred," says Stacy. "We both immediately ran from the forest in opposite directions. I didn't even have time to feel or think anything. My body just all of a sudden sent me running faster than I've ever run in my life."

Stacy insists this type of behavior is extremely unusual for her. She is not the type to scare easily and says the things that frighten most people have never sent her running. "I'm not a skittish person. I don't even get scared in haunted houses at Halloween. Even if someone comes up and scares me or something, I may jump, because I'm shocked at first, but I don't just run for it. Usually I realize what it is, and have time to think 'OK, I'm not really in danger.' But this was just different." Instinctively, she felt whatever spirits she encountered were angry and evil.

A few years later, another family member did up a booklet of Stacy's family history and ancestry. For Stacy, it opened her eyes to the possible truth of her experience. "It went all the way back to the year 1000, which was very exciting. Come to find out, our ancestors had burned down and taken over Ruthin at some point. Could it have been a ghost of one of the people who were killed at that time? Do they somehow know that I am related? That's the best explanation for me." Now that her instinctive sense of homecoming has been validated, Stacy plans to return to the land of her ancestors to stay in some of the other houses and castles in which her forbears lived…and died. True to her word, she has no intention of running scared. She looks forward to meeting her spectral ancestors. "Who knows what other things I may experience!"

# Salzburg Castle
## SALZBURG, AUSTRIA

Salzburg Castle is alive with more than just the memories of *The Sound of Music* being filmed there. It has a spirited life beyond its movie fame. Now if the name Theophrastus Bombastus von Hohenheim doesn't mean anything to you, don't feel badly. Because this ghost also answers to the name Paracelsus—that's the name this visionary 16th-century physician chose for himself.

Born in Switzerland in the late 1400s (the dates range from 1493 to 1498), he moved to Austria as a child, and after training at a mining school decided to become a doctor. He was a wanderer and an independent thinker who swam against the tide of medical thought that supported the humoral theory of disease. Instead he advocated the use of specific remedies for specific diseases. He is credited as the first person to introduce the use of chemicals such as opium, mercury, sulfur and iron into use as medicines. Although his writings contain a strange blend of mystical jargon and sound observation, Paracelsus' work became the foundation for much of modern medicine. But his ego and arrogance earned him as many enemies as it did kudos. He openly scoffed at the widespread practice of bloodletting. He vehemently argued against those who followed the practices of Galen. He was expelled from most major medical schools. And he earned himself a place in linguistic history, because the word bombastic—meaning energetically belligerent—comes from his name. So, it really is no surprise that his sudden, unexplained death was shrouded in mystery.

*The majestic fortress stands on a steep hill and overlooks Salzburg's Old Town.*

Paracelsus had been invited to live at Salzburg Castle by the Archbishop Ernst in 1541 to try to avoid the long list of people who called him an enemy. However, only a few months later he died alone in a small room at the White Horse Inn. No cause of death was revealed and his body was quickly buried in the graveyard of St. Sebastian Church. That might have been the end of the story, except that reports started to emerge from psychics visiting the castle that the energy of Paracelsus still roamed the grounds. Dennis William Hauck, in his international collection of haunted places, found the strongest case to be that of an American tourist who had a life-altering experience after a trip to the castle in 1986. Deb Dupre was followed by a strange mist, which she captured in some of the photos that she took while walking through the grounds. But her contact with such strong spirit energy caused her to change her entire life, exploring alchemy and becoming much more creative and unconventional.

Paranormal experts who have spent time on the castle grounds claim that Paracelsus' spirit is looking for manuscripts that were taken from him and hidden. Many very ill people still visit his gravesite in hopes that his spirit will heal them. Could it be that the lost manuscripts contain an important, lifesaving medical key that modern science has not yet found? Perhaps Paracelsus still believes his work might make a difference in the healing of our sick. If so, we can only hope that those missing manuscripts are eventually found.

# 2
# Government
# & Public
# Places

# Banished!
## NIAMEY, NIGER

You rarely hear of stories of entire cities being haunted, but Niger's capital is apparently so besieged by evil spirits that its mayor went public with the problem. Niamey's mayor, Jules Oguet, told a major international news agency in May 2004 that he ordered "qualified" sorcerers to chase away the nasty entities that have been terrorizing his city's residents.

The sinister specters make their appearances at night. Late night frolickers have filed several complaints of a woman who materializes out of thin air, utters curses and threats, then vanishes. Witnesses say it was as if the spirit evaporated right in front of their eyes. Young, scantily clad women seem to be favorite targets of the malignant spook.

Rather than take the tales lightly, Mayor Oguet responded with what could be called a "war on terror"—West African style. "Given the rumor which has been circulating for at least three weeks now of strange apparitions stalking people, notably women, I have ordered all the elderly chiefs of Niamey to resort to the traditional sacrifices, with qualified people, to stop the curse," the mayor announced.

"People should be reassured: if there are any evil spirits, they will be dealt with." That's what the mayor told people via a local radio station.

Did it work? I have not been able to find out. But witchcraft and belief in spirits is widespread in West Africa and sorcerers are highly influential in communities. If they banished the evil from Niamey's streets, one can only hope the spirits complied and hit the road.

# Ghosts at the White House
## WASHINGTON, DC, USA

*It seems that the White House is haunted. This was a most interesting piece of news to me, for it seemed to me to be the only thing wanting to make the White House the most interesting spot in the United States...*
                    —Archibald Butt to Clara Butt, July 26, 1911

*The damned place is haunted, sure as shootin'...You and Margie had better come back and protect me before some of these ghosts carry me off.*
                    Harry Truman, in a letter to his wife Bess,
                    September 8, 1946

Dead American presidents and their wives—it's an exclusive club. At the White House, the current administration functions in the shadow of the leaders who have gone before. And based on interviews with several staff members, a few of those shadows move about, turn off lights, admonish flower pickers and shut doors. To those who live and work in the White House, the ghosts are as familiar as the building's silhouette. However, the stories may not be as well known to the average person, so I thought it might be worthwhile to include some of the tales here.

In a way, it seems obvious that the building holding so much of the United States' history should be haunted, especially when some of the many presidents housed under its roof died still firmly committed to leading the country. In fact, one of the longtime White House employees, Chief

*Abraham Lincoln usually appears in the White House when he feels the country's security is at risk.*

Usher Gary Walters, said in an online chat session on the White House web site in 2003 that most of the recent presidents feel the presence of their predecessors. "The presidents that I have worked for have all indicated a feeling of the previous occupants of the White House."

The fatal gunshot that killed Abraham Lincoln in 1865 robbed the country of a president, but may have given the White House one of its first ghosts. (He may not have been the very first ghost because Lincoln's wife Mary apparently heard the spirit of Andrew Jackson cursing a blue streak.) Many White House staff claim to have seen the tall, bearded figure inside the building. White House operations foreman Tony Savoy got an early morning jolt that no amount of caffeine could provide. In a 2003 video interview he says, "I was taking care of the plants on the second floor and I suddenly saw President Lincoln sitting in the room with his hands folded and legs crossed." Savoy remembers the moment with remarkable clarity. "He was wearing a charcoal gray pin-striped suit and black spats with three buttons over the side and black shoes." Startled to see the former president sitting there, Tony stopped what he was doing and stared. It's a good thing Tony paused because the ghost of Lincoln appeared only briefly. Savoy recalls, "When I blinked he was gone. I went downstairs and told assistant usher Nelson Pierce what I had seen, and he said I'm just one of the other ones who have seen him over the past years." For Savoy, in that split second, the notion of ghosts flipped from fairy tale to frighteningly real. "Now I believe in it."

Dennis Freemeyer, an assistant usher with 25 years of experience at the White House, also had a strange encounter. Back in the Reagan years, he was filling in for another employee doing the evening rounds, which involved checking to make sure the lights were off. He went to the Lincoln bedroom and turned off the chandelier with the dimmer switch. Dennis then crossed the hallway to go into the Queen's Bedroom. "I was looking into the darkened Lincoln bedroom and saw the lights come on," says Dennis. Knowing all the ghost stories, he actually ran across the hall hoping to catch a glimpse of something. At first he didn't see anything, so he turned the chandelier off again and at that moment realized he was not alone. "I got a very cold chill, I could definitely feel something. I looked around, looked in the mirror thinking maybe there was something behind me, which of course there wasn't, but without a doubt I could feel a very cold presence of someone or something there." Just to be sure it wasn't his imagination playing tricks on him, Dennis confirmed with the White House electrician that the light had not been acting up. So far, Dennis says his incident is the only time that light has ever done that to anybody. "That's my only experience but it's certainly one I've never forgotten."

Gary Walters had his own eerie experience while working on the state floor of the White House. During the online chat, he admitted that one night while working in an area by a staircase there was a very strange rush of cold air. He and some police officers felt it pass between them, moving toward the stairs. Then two doors that stand open all day suddenly closed by themselves. "I have never seen these doors move before without somebody specifically closing them by hand," says Gary. The experience was so odd that he and the officers checked to see if someone had closed another set of doors usually left open to somehow create a vacuum that would cause the doors to close. No other doors were closed. Gary Walters isn't sure if he encountered Lincoln's ghost that day but he does know something extremely strange happened.

Now, according to American folklore, Lincoln has been haunting the White House for decades, most actively through the Roosevelt administration. It is believed he returns when he feels the country's security is at risk. Does that explain his sudden reappearance during 2003? In any event, in the 13 years that Franklin Roosevelt held office, Lincoln apparently monitored events closely. Lincoln's bedroom became a study for the First Lady, Eleanor, and while she never saw his ghost, she did tell people that she felt as if someone were in the room watching. A clerk at the time claimed to walk in on Lincoln pulling on his boots, as if preparing for action. And a shocked Queen Wilhelmina of the Netherlands opened her bedroom door one evening after being awakened by repeated knocking on it and came face to face with the dead president. She fainted. The Queen admitted that her story sounded ridiculous, but said when she saw Lincoln standing there, everything went black.

Who else haunts the White House? During the Taft administration, the ghost of Abigail Adams drifted through the doors of the East Room on her way to hang laundry. And when President Woodrow Wilson's wife asked the gardener to remove some rose bushes, the ghost of former First Lady Dolley Madison gave the gardener a scolding, warning him not to mess with her plants. William Henry Harrison, the ninth president and first to die in office (he succumbed to a vicious cold just 30 days after beginning his presidency) is believed to be the source of strange noises coming from the White House attic.

Really, when you think about it, 1600 Pennsylvania Avenue is just a big, old haunted house, not so different from dozens of haunted homes that dot the continent. It is a distinguished cadre of ghosts, whose pedigree may be a little better than most phantoms, but in the end they keep the people living there on edge no differently than any other house full of ghosts. President Harry Truman often complained of cold drafts and weird popping and creaking noises in the old house, blaming the noisy specters. What might the ghosts of the past be whispering in George W. Bush's ear, I wonder? And do they keep him awake at night?

# Phantom Menace or Presidential Scam?

## LILONGWE, MALAWI

In the opulent, 300-room palace used by Malawi's president, the best security system money can buy apparently doesn't keep out mysterious ghosts or evil spirits. The story came to light when a BBC reporter got wind of the news that President Bingu wa Mutharika moved out of the Lilongwe-based mansion because ghosts terrorized him in his sleep.

Despite the size of the palace, the spirits found Mutharika each night. Malani Mtonga, who counsels the president on religious affairs, revealed to the media that shortly after Mr. Mutharika moved into the monstrous home in December 2004, he began hearing strange noises. Worse yet was the sensation of feeling rats crawling on his bed, only to find nothing there when he turned on the lights. The situation became so frightening that Mtonga said his boss packed up and relocated to a different palace 60 or so miles away in Kasungu. "We have asked clerics from several Christian churches including the Roman Catholic to pray for the new state house to exorcise evil spirits," Mtonga told the BBC.

It's hard to say where the evil spirits originated. Malawi's former president Kamuzu Banda built the palatial abode on some 1400 acres of land outside the capital, but after waiting 20 years to move in (that's how long it took to build the place) Mr. Banda moved out after only 90 days. Could he too have been haunted by nasty spirits? Or perhaps he just suffered from a stinging conscience as a result of spending so much money on himself while many people in Malawi lived in poverty. No one else chose to live in the presidential palace, and until Mr. Mutharika moved in, it housed Malawi's parliament.

Interestingly, soon after the story became public Bingu wa Mutharika flatly denied that he moved out because of any ghosts. He even had the reporters who told the story arrested. But it's not every day the president of a country confronts the paranormal, so perhaps he simply didn't want to be seen by his peers and countrymen as a scaredy-cat!

# Sao Paulo City Hall
## SAO PAULO, BRAZIL

Administering to a city of 20 million people would be enough to give any municipal worker nightmares, but add to that a haunted workplace and Sao Paolo's city councilors really do deserve a little extra sympathy. Council members and support staff in the 12-story city council building say they're in no doubt the place is haunted. They have reported dozens of paranormal events, from seeing ghosts that appear to be normal people but dissolve like mist in sunshine, to hearing footsteps, seeing lights and being plagued by phones that ring with no one on the other end.

In Dennis Hauck's *International Directory of Haunted Places*, one council member claims he and his staff were locked in the building late one night after working past midnight. They wrapped up their session and tried to exit but found the door to their room jammed shut. This situation was extremely odd, given that the door locked from the inside. When the group then heard strange voices and furniture moving on the other side of the door, they called security for help. The guard arrived moments later and easily opened the door. He confirmed that no one else was in the building.

Naturally, ghost hunters and international television crews for paranormal programs arrive on the City Hall doorstep looking to explain this phenomenon, or at the very least capture one of the many ghostly figures on videotape. There don't seem to be any conclusive answers. One theory suggests that the ghosts are connected to the February 1974 fire in a newly built skyscraper close to City Hall, which killed 220 people. The fire trapped dozens of people on higher floors and many people jumped to their death rather than face the flames. Under Sao Paulo's emergency service plan, the City Hall immediately transformed to a makeshift morgue. It makes sense that there would be some souls wandering about the halls, possibly still unaware that they are dead and not sure how they ended up trapped in their municipal government offices. (Now that might be some people's idea of hell!)

Other paranormal investigators determined after a lengthy visit in 1999 that the spirits were merely the manifestation of poltergeist energy created by disturbed employees.

But many people believe the problem is much older, and goes much deeper—right to the core of Brazil's evolution as a nation. Some psychics say the energy is that of ancient spirits, not dead office workers or unhappy civic employees. The colonists of Brazil apparently tread not so carefully when they took over much of the land and built on sacred burial grounds, including the current site for the City Hall. The area has been called the Vale do Anhangabau, or the Valley of Spirits. Could the phantoms in Sao Paolo's city council building be the disturbed souls of native South Americans still upset over centuries of mistreatment and enslavement? Could they be prodding current councilors to make amends or to ensure better treatment for all indigenous peoples in the future?

# Terror in the Tunisian Embassy
## Moscow, Russia

The haunting in the historic Russian building that served as the Tunisian Embassy started with a water leak. To be more precise, it started when the work crew began digging to find the source of the leak. But this haunting was not the usual ghost made a little cranky by some repair work kind of situation. This was awful. Horrific. Frightening. And very, very disturbing.

The prominent 19th-century building sits on a tiny street a few blocks north of the Kremlin. Despite the proximity to Moscow's bustling downtown and major roads, this little residential street maintains an air of subdued grandeur. The embassy started out as home to Count Orloff's mistress until it became property of the state during the Bolshevik Revolution. After that, it was almost like a hotel or military home, with a stream of upper echelon party members living in it. In the 1950s, Tunisia was given the property to use as an embassy.

In 40 years, no one who visited the beautiful building with its gold-plated toilets and mahogany furniture ever commented on the presence of ghosts. No one complained of hearing moans or seeing apparitions of scared children run through the halls. The only stories that were told suggested the embassy was both luxurious and peaceful. That all changed in 1998 once the hot water line started to leak.

The city workers arrived one spring day to start digging in search of the leak. Because of the way water in Moscow is delivered, from a central plant to certain areas via insulated pipes contained in underground, cement-lined conduits, the only information from a pressure test was that the main line to the Tunisian Embassy had a leak somewhere on the grounds. Exactly *where* that leak was still needed to be determined. And since these water lines had not been touched since installation in 1949, that meant digging up sections, checking for the leak, then moving on to the next length of pipe. The workers began systematically, starting from the outer edge of the embassy grounds and moving inward toward the building. The ghosts showed up the first night, almost as if they were awakened by the clanging of shovels on concrete.

The ambassador's wife saw the first ghost late in the evening while on her way to use the second-floor washroom. What she saw shocked her both as a Muslim and as a mother. A pretty, blond young girl ran toward her, naked and terrified, her mouth open in a silent scream. Frozen in her tracks, the ambassador's wife watched as the petrified teen raced past her, leaving a wake of icy air swirling around the speechless woman, then vanished into thin air at the end of the hall. The next morning she told her husband of the vision, emphasizing that the girl, who looked to be about 14, was stark naked and seemed to be oblivious to that fact. The ambassador assumed it was just a vivid nightmare. Wrong.

The same thing happened the next night to a completely different witness in another part of the house. For three nights, people living in the embassy claimed to see different naked, terrified teenaged girls running down the halls, screaming but without sound as if part of some silent horror film, then suddenly disappearing. The cook apparently saw two ghoulish girls at once while on her way to the kitchen to make breakfast. Six incidents of seeing the apparitions were recorded. Then there were the horrible cries for help, young girls' voices crying for their mothers or for salvation. Naturally, no one at the embassy was getting much sleep.

After five days of intense haunting, the Tunisian Embassy staff was about ready to pack up and move home. No one could explain the dramatic shift in energy in the building. The horrific sights and sounds made everyone dread nightfall. Meanwhile the city's water crew was unaware of the problems going on inside the embassy; they just kept showing up each morning, digging up another section of pipe, and going home at the end of the day not having found the source of the water leak.

Everything became clear only when the crew of the Moscow City Water Department arrived to dig up the last section of pipe, the one closest to the embassy. It was May 16, and when they pulled the cement casing off the pipes, they found the leak. They also found six sets of bones. Six bodies were lying on either side of the water pipe, all young girls between the ages of 12 and 18. An examination of the remains revealed they had all been shot through the head and were buried naked along with the cement conduit when it was initially placed seven feet underground in 1949. There was nothing to identify the girls. A caustic substance had been placed on their bodies to ensure they decomposed quickly. In 1949, when that hot water line was installed, the home was occupied by the director of the Soviet Union's secret police, Lavrenti Beria, Minister of Internal Affairs. Was it the girls' spirits that somehow created the water leak to bring their murder to light?

Perhaps this comes as no surprise, but no further investigation was done. The bodies were removed and buried elsewhere. The leak was repaired. The embassy staff moved across the city to another location. Apparently, the sightings ended after the girls' remains received a proper burial, but the embassy people were only there for four weeks before moving out. Since then, the building has been empty. Or is it? Could the girls' frightened ghosts still run through the halls, not screaming to be found any longer, but crying out for justice?

# The Kremlin's Terrible Ghost
## MOSCOW, RUSSIA

Ghosts love Russia's Kremlin. There's Ivan the Terrible, another former czar, Lenin and Lenin's would-be assassin all keeping company in Moscow's almost mythic self-contained city. Stories are told of seeing shadows, hearing footsteps and witnessing apparitions in various parts of the many-faceted government center. Many of the ghosts have one thing in common—they make it a point to show up just before things turn bad for whoever sees them.

The ghost of Ivan the Terrible, Russia's most unpopular and brutal czar, is said to bode disaster for Russian rulers. Some reports say his large shadow roams through the lower level of the bell tower that bears his name. Other accounts refer to his unsightly, horrifying appearance; his face is covered in fire and he wields a massive baton. Ivan the Terrible ruled through the mid-1500s and history is divided on his contribution. Many believe he was mad, but it is certain that he was violent and cruel. He personally tortured his captives, sentenced thousands to exile and beat his own son to death. Despite his pre-death transformation (he was re-christened as a monk and buried in a monk's habit), seeing his ghost would not likely warm people's hearts. Nicholas II, the last of the czars, wrote in his memoirs about seeing Ivan the Terrible on the eve of his crowning ceremony in 1894. Nicholas and Empress Alexandra Fydorovna both saw Ivan's awful figure, and the czar noted that they both took it to be a very bad sign. (Nicholas abdicated in 1917 under pressure of political reformists. He and his family were shipped to Siberia, where

*Ivan the Terrible*

the Bolsheviks murdered them.) The faded specter of Ivan the Terrible has also been seen walking a lone vigil through the Kremlin and some people speculate that the tyrant is in search of his wife and his son, tormented by the guilt of his own actions.

Some of the Kremlin's other towers are haunted as well. A wall of the Konstantino-Eleninskaya Tower occasionally glows red in one spot in an area that was once a torture chamber during the 17th century. In Komendantskaya Tower, the ghost of Fanny Kaplan still holds the gun she planned to use to kill Lenin. Witnesses claim to have seen a pale woman with messy hair carrying a gun. Or perhaps Fanny's spirit carries the gun that ended her life, as she was executed for her murderous intentions by one of the Kremlin's superintendents.

Out on the Kremlin's wall, would-be czar Dmitry the Pretender caught people by surprise by appearing in 1991. This appearance would come as quite a shock given he was assassinated in 1606 by the boyars (nobles). As well, the False Dmitry gets credit in Russian history as precipitating what is known as the "Time of Troubles." So, seeing him gesturing and giving signs to the people should have set off some alarm bells. It didn't. But the following day, people awoke to news of a coup ousting Soviet leader Mikhail Gorbachev. The coup was soon crushed but the August 19 attempted power grab did ultimately hasten the end of the Soviet Union. Perhaps the next time Dmitry appears on the Kremlin wall, observers will pay more attention.

Lenin's ghost appeared as recently as 1993, though he started communicating from beyond the grave in the early 1960s. He contacted a local psychic to express his displeasure at being placed in a public mausoleum next to the body of Stalin. Lying in state was bad enough, but to be stuck beside a man who nearly destroyed the Communist Party grated on his ghostly nerves. The woman delivered Lenin's message at the 22nd Congress of the Communist Party and within

*Ghosts love Russia's Kremlin.*

24 hours Stalin's body mysteriously disappeared from the Red Square mausoleum, leaving Lenin alone to "receive" the public. Lenin also is thought to be behind various strange poltergeist-type incidents involving things moving in the Kremlin. Ironically, the collapse of the USSR and the Communist government in 1993 prompted Lenin's ghost to reappear, pacing anxiously in his old office. Since he couldn't roll in his grave, being out on display as he was, maybe that was the only way for his vexed spirit to burn off a little steam.

# Visions at Versailles
## PARIS, FRANCE

Paris, 1901. Two English academics stroll through the gardens at the Palace of Versailles, gossiping about people they know and meandering through the sprawling complex on their way to the Petit Trianon. In a turn-of-the-century take on "a funny thing happened on the way to the Forum..." these teachers slipped into a time warp and without realizing it, walked along paths that had ceased to exist for more than 100 years. Along the way they bumped into the ghosts of Marie Antoinette and members of her court. The mystical experience of Anne Moberly and Eleanor Jourdain, and their infamous account of what happened, turned their world inside out. It also launched one of the most famous—and ongoing—controversies over whether Versailles is haunted.

What happened to the vacationing schoolteachers? This is their story in a rather large nutshell. On August 10, 1901, the pair toured the palace at Versailles, and then went in search of the Petit Trianon but lost their way. They admitted in their 1911 published account, *An Adventure*, that they "began talking about our mutual acquaintances in England and paid but little attention to our surroundings." They passed a deserted farmhouse and an old plough lying on the side of the road, eventually finding an entrance to the garden. As they entered, Anne Moberly suddenly felt overwhelmed by "an extraordinary depression." Her companion would later confirm that she too felt a "depression and loneliness" about the area. Both sensed an eerie oppressiveness to the garden despite being outdoors, and noted that the world suddenly seemed flat,

*Visitors to the Petit Trianon have been known to wander into unexpected territory.*

almost two-dimensional, according to Rosemary Guiley's *Encyclopedia of Ghosts and Spirits.* As they continued to walk, Anne and Eleanor saw two men dressed in "long grayish-green coats with small three-cornered hats." Anne assumed they were gardeners because one carried a spade. The lost women asked for directions and were instructed to continue directly down the path in front of them. They soon came upon a gazebo shaded by trees where a "repulsive" man with a pockmarked face sat in the gloom of the shadows. Silently he stared at Anne and Eleanor. Both women instantly disliked the unpleasant man, and they moved quickly to put distance between him and them. Just then, another man ran up behind them, speaking rapid French in a strange accent, which they could barely understand. Anne Moberly made out that he seemed to be giving directions to the house, indicating they should turn right and cross a bridge. This fellow too must be a gardener, they thought, though when they looked for him again he had vanished. Moments later, they arrived at the garden by the back of the Petit Trianon. Anne saw a woman sitting on a stool, sketching or reading. She described the woman later as having "a good deal of fair hair that fluffed around her forehead. Her light summer dress was arranged on her shoulders in handkerchief fashion and there was a little line of either green or gold near the edge of the handkerchief...I thought she was a tourist, but that her dress was old-fashioned and rather unusual." It would come as a surprise to Anne to learn that Eleanor did not see the woman. Suddenly, a young man came running out of a nearby doorway, slamming the door behind him. He told them the front of the house was on the other side of the building, so Anne and Eleanor walked around to the front of the Petit Trianon where they both felt the dark, oppressive mood lift and the world return to vibrant, three-dimensions.

Almost as strange as that experience was is the fact that neither woman spoke of her experiences at Versailles for several days. When they finally compared notes, Anne happened to mention the sketching woman. Eleanor declared she had not seen anyone in the garden. They began to realize something strange and supernatural had likely taken place, so they agreed to write down separate accounts of what had happened while out walking. After comparing notes, they concluded the Petit Trianon was haunted and surmised that they had actually traveled back in time 109 years to relive the memories of Marie Antoinette on the day that she was imprisoned: August 10, 1792. As if to verify her assumption, Anne Moberly stumbled across a picture of the queen drawn by an artist named Wertmüller. Right down to the clothes, it was the same woman she had seen in the garden.

When Eleanor asked around to find out if anyone had heard stories about Versailles being haunted, she was told by one friend that it was well known that on a certain day in August, Marie Antoinette could be seen sitting outside the Petit Trianon. As a bit of background, the Petit Trianon was commissioned by Louis XV in 1762 and was finished in 1770. When the king died in 1774, his grandson Louis XVI gave the house to his queen, Marie Antoinette, as a private getaway. During the French Revolution, when the monarchy was despised by the starving citizens as arrogant and uncaring, Marie Antoinette and Louis were taken from Versailles by an angry mob and forced to live at the royal palace in Paris. In 1792 the king and queen were imprisoned; the date of their imprisonment was August 10—the same day as Eleanor and Anne's visit to the gardens of Versailles. Louis was beheaded in January 1793; Marie Antoinette followed him to the scaffold in October of that year.

Intrigued by this mystery, the two women made several trips back to Versailles over the next decade to find a plausible explanation for their experience. What they found only raised more questions. Eleanor Jourdain returned in January 1902 and felt that same depressing, eerie sensation come over her. She saw two men dressed in tunics and capes with hoods lifting wood into a cart. She glanced away for a moment, and when she looked back the men were a long way in the distance. Jourdain and Moberly returned together in 1904 and to their astonishment, they could not retrace their earlier route. The gazebo and bridge did not exist. An enormous rhododendron bush grew where the woman had sat sketching. Tourists filled every nook and cranny, unlike the empty grounds with only a handful of people that they had seen. How could it be that they had missed seeing all these tourists? And what happened to the bridge and gazebo?

Digging even deeper, the women found documents, maps and other evidence that suggested they had somehow tripped back in time. They felt quite sure that the scene they witnessed existed in 1789, and they put forth this theory: they had somehow entered a lingering memory of Queen Marie Antoinette. As proof, they wrote in their book that the plough they had seen, which no longer sat on the grounds, had been on display in 1789. The missing bridge had been there in 1789, and a gazebo-like building was shown on an old map as being at the location where they encountered it, though it had been torn down many years prior to 1901. The men in green coats wore uniforms that matched the soldiers who guarded Marie Antoinette. The sinister man with the scarred face closely resembled the Comte de Vaudreuil, an associate of the queen's who had suffered smallpox. The door of the house that the footman had banged shut had actually been boarded shut for years.

*An Adventure*, written under the pseudonyms Miss Morison and Miss Lamont, drew out more stories of strange goings-on at Versailles. It also drew some savage salvos from critics who debunked the women's story by saying the entire premise of their "research" did not hold water. Eleanor Sidgwick of the Society for Psychical Research in London essentially wrote the tale off as a trick of memory. She pointed out that the women even admitted they weren't paying close attention, so they might easily have seen real people and mistaken them as ghosts. Other critics went after Moberly and Jourdain's argument that there was no way they could have known about the details of Versailles in 1789 and that their recollection was proof of either ghosts or time travel. But skeptics discovered the women didn't write the book until many months after their experience, and then added many of their book's details in 1906, well after conducting their research. There was enough doubt cast on the accuracy of their description to suggest the story was a product of Anne and Eleanor's imaginations.

However, the story doesn't end there. The British spinsters were the first to go public with their strange story of ghosts on the royal grounds, but they would not be the last. Ghostly reports continued to emerge from Versailles. In 1928 Clare Burrow felt a strange depression during her visit to the Petit Trianon. She and her companion Ann Lambert saw an old man wearing an unusual silver and green uniform. When they asked for directions, he shouted some odd, unintelligible words in French and then suddenly vanished. They also witnessed other people in period clothing, but it wasn't until

Burrow read *An Adventure* some time later that she realized she had experienced a haunting. There are several other accounts from witnesses who saw people in period dress. In most cases, the people in the old-fashioned clothing seem to be there one minute, and disappear the next. A woman named Elizabeth Hatton watched a man and woman wearing peasant clothes from another time vanish before her eyes during a visit to Versailles in 1938. A London lawyer and his wife walked through the grounds in May 1955 right after a heavy thunderstorm. The wife had that same feeling of depression come over her as Eleanor and Anne described. As they walked along, they saw two men and a woman wearing colorful period costumes. Though preoccupied with their own conversation, the lawyer and his wife reported that they suddenly realized the trio had vanished—they disappeared in an area where there was nowhere to hide.

Experts can't agree about the authenticity of Versailles' ghosts. On one hand, it has been noted that these odd occurrences take place in a public park where people often arrive dressed in period clothing from the time of Louis XVI's court. On the other hand, many of the eyewitness accounts give details that are consistent with known facts about the people who populated the Petit Trianon during the late 1770s.

Whatever the case, more hauntings keep being reported over the years. One theory is that Versailles became a center of emotional power—energy trapped in the area by the former inhabitants who loved it so dearly but knew they were witnessing the end of an era. Perhaps those sensitive to it walk into a vortex of memories and briefly relive moments of a time long past. What really happened at Versailles? The truth may be out there, but as yet no one has found it.

# Dalkeith Fire Station
## DALKEITH, LOTHIAN, SCOTLAND

In the Midlothian village of Dalkeith, in the east of Scotland, a four-alarm crisis of supernatural proportions moved the commander of the fire station to call for backup. Bob Wotherspoon and his team of fire fighters were being terrorized by a ghostly monk that wandered throughout the hall. In an article in the *Edinburgh Evening News* dated January 29, 2005, firefighters complained of hearing "strange voices, eerie screams and loud bangs in the middle of the night." The crew isn't surprised that their fire station is haunted, given that it is built on the site of a ruined abbey known for its ghost sightings since the 18th century. There has also been a lot of excavation work done lately, which tends to churn up the spirit world. However, knowing you may have a ghost and actually dealing with one on a day-to-day basis are very different things. Commander Wotherspoon finally called the Angels Gateway Spiritualist Church in Bilston to help get rid of their menacing monk. He rationalized the move in an interview with *The Scotsman*'s Simon Pia saying, "People who haven't seen it for themselves have been saying it's a lot of nonsense, so we always say the same thing—come and spend a night here. But no one has taken us up on our offer."

Ada Donaldson, the Angels Gateway leader, answered the call for help. Initially, she and another woman visited the fire station to determine the exact nature of the problem. "I gave them a quick reading," she told me, "and found there were a number of spirits in there, but only one that was causing the trouble." Ada tuned in quickly to the spirit of a former monk named Thomas Howard who as a boy had been raised by the members of the abbey and then became a monk himself. "However, he dabbled in the black arts," Ada explained in hushed tones. "He was a fairly evil spirit who had done some very evil things in his life." His penchant for making people fearful did not diminish with death. Ada told me that Thomas Howard had altered the energy in the fire station, which explained why the firefighters sensed keenly the presence of a dark shadow and felt a general uneasiness about their workplace. "If a spirit invokes fear, it can feed on it."

She and 11 other church members arrived at the fire station on the evening of January 23, 2005 to carry out a special banishment ceremony. Using Ouija boards, they contacted the phantom monk. The spirit of Thomas Howard arrived and then spent most of the vigil explaining himself, his life story and the stories of how he caused the violent deaths of many people. Ada said that at one point during the banishment ceremony, he became so strong that he manipulated her into a kneeling position and she felt her hands crossed in front of her as if they were being tied. "He wanted us to know what he had done to his victims," she said, without going into the gory details. Eventually, the group was able to instruct the ghost monk to leave the station and cross into the light. Ada is sure he left because he was ready to go. "He just wanted his story to be known first." All is now quiet at the fire station, and the only alarms going off are in aid of the citizens of Dalkeith.

# Middlesbrough Ambulance Station

## MIDDLESBROUGH, NORTH YORKSHIRE, ENGLAND

Exorcism proved to be the only route for the employees at the recently closed ambulance base in the Tees, East and North Yorkshire Ambulance Service. The Middlesbrough Ambulance Station served the community for more than 50 years (it was replaced by a bigger, more modern facility), and though the people who worked there bid it an emotional farewell in September 2004, there was one aspect on which they seemed fairly happy to lock the doors. The staff there did not embrace the ghosts. No warm fuzzies occur at the thought of running into either the "Man in the Gray Suit," as they nicknamed the one phantom, or the smoky gray apparition seen floating around the station yard.

Allan Grieff, an operational supervisor with 12 years of experience at Middlesbrough, told the *Evening Gazette* that it is believed the ghosts picked their station because of its proximity to the graveyard next door. The mysterious gray-suited figure first appeared in the 1960s, wandering through the halls at night, terrifying the crew on late shift. Grieff says many of the workers claim to have seen it. "He appears and disappears in a couple of seconds, usually in the corridor outside the offices, but he has been seen in the kitchen," he told the *Gazette*. Perhaps that's just a case of mass delusion as some skeptics believe, but it is hard to deny the security camera videotapes that show a smoky grayish figure moving about the station on more than one occasion. The wraith even "walked" right through one of the ambulance station employees! After witnessing that, the staff wanted no more of the ghost in their workplace and they called on a local church minister to come and perform a ritualistic exorcism. That seemed to do the trick, because no one saw the ghost after that. But that is only one of the two spirits accounted for—is the Man in the Gray Suit still at large?

# 3
# Homes

# No. 12 Deanery Lane
## PIETERMARITZBURG, KWAZULU-NATAL, SOUTH AFRICA

It is one thing to discover your house is haunted, but it is quite another to have the ghost lecture you on your lifestyle, your housekeeping and even the people to whom you lend things. That situation confronts a young couple living in the house at No. 12 Deanery Lane in Pietermaritzburg. Even rarer is that the people who live nearby have recognized their old neighbor as the ghost lecturer and say she has returned thousands of miles to her home just to keep an eye on things.

It seems the ghost that haunts Moses Caluza and his partner Mia Venter in their Deanery Lane home is none other than the late historian Ruth Gordon. Ruth lived most of her life in Pietermaritzburg but returned to England at the age of 87. As she left, Ruth declared it would take some serious machinery to dig up her roots and shift them out of the KwaZulu-Natal capital city. Ruth obviously knew what she was talking about because four years later she died, and not long after that she showed up on the sofa at No. 12 wearing a gray apron and full of pent-up frustration that she unleashed on the unwitting Mia Venter. Mia told her story to the *Natal Witness* saying, "She took me for her daughter and started telling me how she was forced to leave the city, how she never wanted to sell her home. I froze like a block of ice."

Suddenly, all the weird things that had been happening since Mia and Moses moved into the house started making sense. They had noticed strange creaking on the floors and other odd sounds, and the stove kept being turned off. Apparently Gordon's ghost thought they were being wasteful. The unhappy spirit also told the couple that she was not pleased with their living arrangement, given they are not married and have a four-year-old son. And that's not all. It seems once you let a ghost have the floor, it makes sure that it uses every square inch. Venter heard from the former owner that she disapproved of them taking in lodgers. She also was keeping an otherworldly eye on things in the house as if they still belonged to her and chided Mia for loaning out the stepladder, insisting it be returned immediately. Now that is ghoulish chutzpah.

After the sofa tongue-lashing, Moses Caluza contacted local ghost experts to find out how to deal with the busybody apparition. He also called Gordon's daughters in England to see if it was indeed her spirit that felt the need to watch their every move. They confirmed that the sharp-tongued specter closely resembled their deceased mother. Shirley Gault, who lives farther down Deanery Lane and knew Ruth Gordon when she was alive, told Moses and Mia that her friend had obviously returned to the house she loved so well. "Ruth never wanted to leave Pietermaritzburg, although she did put on a brave face about it," Shirley told the local paper.

Paranormal experts say it's not surprising that the elderly woman's ghost made its way across the ocean back to Deanery Lane. In the spirit world, there is no such thing as distance. So, to create a little peace within their home, Moses and Mia followed the advice of a psychic. A little strategically placed holy water seems to have done the trick in keeping the nattering wraith at bay. Now all they have to do is try to forget that the spirit of a 91-year-old woman keeps trying to peer into every corner of their lives!

# Plas Teg

## PONTBLYDDYN, NEAR MOLD, FLINTSHIRE, WALES

One of the most famous haunted houses in North Wales is Plas Teg. The restored Jacobean mansion stands just off the busy dual carriageway between Mold and Wrexham at Pontblyddyn. Several ghosts including a notoriously stern judge and a young girl who drowned in a well haunt the 17th-century manor house. Visitors hear footsteps, see misty apparitions and sense an unhappy, otherworldly presence in several of the mansion's rooms. The house has such a reputation for ghosts that it is part of an ongoing study by the Cheshire Paranormal Society, which has been given sole carte blanche by the owner to investigate the various spooky happenings.

John Trevor built the huge square-shaped mansion in 1610 and over the years the unique three-story structure was filled with important antiques and textiles. But in recent times, Plas Teg stood empty, a brooding ominous derelict that definitely looked the part of the scary haunted house at night. Then antique dealer and interior designer Cornelia Bayley bought Plas Teg Hall almost 20 years ago with a dream of restoring the building to its original splendid state, bringing back the beautiful wall hangings, furniture and art that once decorated the many rooms. She also gave the ghosts a much more public stage on which to perform in April 2004 by opening the house every Sunday to visitors as a way of covering the massive cost of restoration.

Who are the ghosts at Plas Teg? One of the main spirits dates right back to the time of the original owner; the daughter of the house died falling down a well. That's the short story and certainly doesn't explain why her spirit remains to roam through the house and gardens. According to ghost investigator and author Richard Holland, the girl fell to her death in the midst of a plan to run away and escape an arranged marriage. It's generally assumed that the maiden was John Trevor's daughter Dorothy, but she could also have been the daughter of the Dacre family who lived in the hall. Although it is unclear as to what exactly took place on the day of her death, the consensus among the various versions of the story is that the girl's parents agreed she would marry an older wealthy man but the girl had fallen in love with a poor farm boy. To avoid a loveless union, the girl arranged to elope with her beloved on the eve before the wedding. She never arrived at the secret location and it was some weeks later before her decomposing body was found at the bottom of the Plas Teg well alongside a bag full of the family's jewels. The girl may have been willing to marry for love, but it appears she had no desire to live on a pauper's wage. She had stolen enough jewels to live comfortably and apparently tumbled into the well and drowned while trying to hide them. Meanwhile, her lover had been unable to cope with both his broken heart and the accusations aimed at him over the girl's disappearance. He hanged himself from a branch on the tree where they had planned to meet. Since then, the girl's spirit and that of her farm boy continue to haunt Plas Teg, something Cornelia Bayley discovered soon after moving in.

One night, she heard the soft tread of a woman walking about on the upper floor. Then, to her surprise, she also heard the pounding thud of a much heavier person coming down the stairs followed by some intense pounding on her bedroom door. When she investigated, there was no one else in the house.

Another of the well-known ghosts believed to haunt Plas Teg is the hard-hearted judge who lived in the manor. George Jeffreys, born May 15, 1648 in nearby Wrexham, chose law as his career path and worked his way right to the top, becoming Lord Chief Justice of England at age 33. He was appointed Solicitor General to the Duke of York, subsequently James II, and also received his knighthood in 1677. During the famous trials for supporters of the Duke of Monmouth, Judge Jeffreys presided. His harsh sentences of death by hanging resulted in the obvious nickname "Hanging Judge Jeffreys." While it has nothing to do with the ghost aspect, for interest's sake it is worth noting that Jeffreys was moved to the Tower of London in 1688 for his safety when James II fled the country. A year later he died there of kidney disease. So the "Hanging Judge" died a virtual prisoner in another city yet his spirit returned to this Welsh mansion to inflect itself on the living. Why would that be? There is no obvious answer. Medium Carl Fletcher, on a tour of the manor recorded by the BBC, noted upon entering the judge's former room that it "has a strange energy in the center, uncomfortable sickly, then a finality, nothing." Fletcher felt that the room doubled as a hanging room. He also picked up that every person who died at the end of a noose may not have been assumed innocent until proven guilty. Is it possible that Judge Jeffreys is remorseful about his sentences, and spends time on this plane as punishment for his decisions?

During his visit to the house, Carl Fletcher claims to have encountered several other spirits. While in the entrance hall, he told the BBC Wales web site, "My hand went ice cold, I could 'see' a child, almost as Alice in the famous *Wonderland* books; blonde curly hair and smock-type dress with deep frills and cuffs and hem." He also saw a female figure in a long blue dress as he made his way up the staircase, discovering later the same woman in a portrait of the Trevor family. It was the daughter who drowned after falling in love "beneath her station." Fletcher claims he heard the voice of a former cook whose spirit is still concerned with feeding those in the house. And curiously, the medium says he felt the presence of the original owner, Sir John Trevor, still angry at his rebellious daughter and tormented by the death of his strong-willed wife who, according to Fletcher, died after a nasty argument and was found dead under the bed in their room.

As I noted at the outset, only one paranormal research group is allowed access to Plas Teg and its ghosts. The Cheshire Paranormal Society (CPS) takes the responsibility of recording and investigating the many spirits quite seriously. Chairman John Millington says there have been several sightings in the hall. "Mediums have come here and ran," he told the BBC. "It's very active and it has been for many years. We've been very successful in what we've been getting."

The CPS corroborated Carl Fletcher's findings that Sir John Trevor's bedroom, known as the Regency Room, is the most palpably haunted room in the manor. But their research suggests Sir John was the fifth squire to live in the hall, around 1742, and that he found out his wife had been cheating on him. He flew into a rage, and his wife's body was later found dead, under what they call "mysterious conditions." For some reason, Sir John drove his horse and trap around the grounds like a madman until he had a bad accident that left him seriously injured. He was bedridden in the Regency Room and died there a month later. Was it his angry state of mind that kept him tied to this plane? His spirit has been seen standing at the end of the bed, a shadowy shape visible when people walk by the door. Other visitors claim to have felt a force push past them or grab them as they were on their way out of the room.

The road that runs past the mansion is equally haunted and somewhat more dangerous. Several ghosts, including the "White Lady," walk up and down the road outside the hall. Misty white shapes appear out of nowhere, forcing many startled drivers to slam on the brakes and swerve sharply outside Plas Teg, convinced that they have run someone over. No body or injured person has ever been found. So should you find yourself cruising the A541 in North Wales and come upon Pontblyddyn, it may be a good idea to slow down. If it's a weekend, it would be worth it to stop and make a trip to see Plas Teg's ghosts for yourself.

# The White Lady
# of Samlesbury Hall
## PRESTON, LANCASHIRE, ENGLAND

There are several people in Lancashire who would argue the 15th-century black and white timber mansion in Preston called Samlesbury Hall should take top honors for most haunted hall in the United Kingdom. The ghost of a woman in white walks the halls and often cries over the love that was torn from her by her family over four centuries ago. Visitors hear the sound of her weeping and the rustle of her skirts as she walks the long halls still grieving and forlorn.

Religion can keep couples apart even in the 21st century, but in the late 1500s to be of differing faiths could be fatal. Unfortunately for Lady Dorothy Southworth, her family's adherence to Catholicism meant her love affair with a young Protestant lad was doomed. The legend of the star-crossed lovers adheres to the hall like ancient moss. The most popular version seems to be based on an 1875 book entitled *Legends and Traditions in Lancashire*. In this book T.T. Wilkinson writes that Sir John Southworth flew into a rage when his daughter asked to be married to, in his eyes, "the son of a family which had deserted its ancestral faith." In lieu of parental consent the young couple planned to elope, but one of Dorothy's brothers discovered the plan and on the appointed night ambushed the couple as they tried to sneak away. Dorothy's lover and a friend who accompanied him were both killed. The Southworth family hid the corpses in the Hall chapel and sent poor Dorothy off to a convent where, according to Wilkinson, "Her mind at last gave away. The name of her murdered lover was ever on her lips, and she died a raving maniac."

By 1875 locals were already reporting seeing a white-gowned woman walking on the grounds, arriving at a spot where her lover met her on bended knee, and then going for a spectral stroll together around the property. The story soon changed to reports of a phantom woman crying within Samlesbury Hall. On February 26, 1926, *The Northern Daily Telegraph* reprinted a letter from an aging colonel who had written to the *London Morning Post*. The colonel detailed his experience at Samlesbury Hall during the Lancashire cotton riots of 1878 when he and his soldiers were stationed there. During the night, the colonel woke to the sound of a woman sobbing inconsolably and though he tried to locate the person, he found no one and went back to bed assuming it was someone sleeping upstairs. The next day when he told his hosts of the strange sounds, they told him a similar version of the legend, except that Dorothy supposedly threw herself out her bedroom window and died.

To add weight to the stories, it had been rumored that the bones of two men were found buried on the property, and Samlesbury historian Robert Eaton may have found the necessary proof. In *Stories of Samlesbury* he tells of how Abram Sharples worked at the hall until 1879, employed by William Harrison. While digging to put in a land drain, Sharples and another fellow named Jacob Baron "unexpectedly broke into an enclosed brick chamber lying just outside the garden wall…The remains of two human bodies were found, which soon fell away to little more than bones and hair." Mr. Harrison apparently resealed the vault with the bones inside.

Mr. Sharples also remembered the cotton riots and that an officer and several dozen soldiers boarded at the hall in 1878—serving to confirm the elderly colonel's story.

In 1940 a caretaker working at the hall took it upon himself to prove whether the ghost stories contained even a smattering of truth. Edward Smith sat up for several nights with a companion and nothing strange occurred. He decided to give it one more night, so on the evening of January 10, the two men held a vigil on the upper floor of the hall. At a quarter to midnight, as they were about to call it a night, they spotted a gray figure moving along the wall toward the fireplace. The apparition paused before the hearth, and then vanished as the men stared in disbelief.

Other spooky stories from the 1940s and 1950s included in Robert Eaton's collection include a sighting of the white-gowned ghost by actors performing in a production at the hall. The cast of the play, appropriately titled "The Tragedy at the House of Southworth," saw a figure pass by the dressing room and at first assumed it was one of the troupe but a head count showed no one was missing. A couple visiting the area claimed they were passed by a female ghost wearing a mackintosh while walking near the hall. They didn't realize it was a ghost until later, when it dawned on them that the woman passed in the dark between the man and his dog who was on a tight leash. Anyone with two feet on the ground would most certainly have tripped over the dog's lead. And a local bus driver stopped to pick up a woman who seemed to be waiting for the bus, but when the doors opened, no one was there. Others saw an apparition walking along the outskirts of the hall in the impression where an old moat once stood.

More recently, staff members at the hall were startled one night when the intruder alarm system turned on repeatedly, despite having been turned off to accommodate an investigation by two psychic mediums. Technicians were summoned, but they couldn't find any reason for the malfunction, or why it happened at consistent intervals. They even questioned the psychics to see if they had brought equipment that might trigger the alarm but found nothing. The alarm continued to sound every seven seconds, and another search proved to be fruitless. Eventually everyone concluded that the ghost was just having a night of fun at their expense.

The woman who runs events at the hall has noted many strange occurrences during her years working in the huge manor. Sylvia Thomas says batteries in cameras and recording equipment routinely lose their charge, going dead within minutes of being in the building. Some visitors claim to feel short of breath while walking through the upper floors, particularly in the Priest Room and the Long Gallery. And then there is just that pervasive atmosphere of something present—unseen, unhappy and otherworldly.

Ironically, the same religious intolerance that fuels this legend may be the reason the story was fabricated in the first place, because at the time when Sir John denounced Protestants as heretics, King Henry VIII reigned and Catholics were being prosecuted in England. Historians have turned up evidence that Samlesbury Hall housed priests and was a secret site for Masses at a time when the service could result in burning at the stake. So a good ghost story might have been a diversion from the truth and a way to keep prying eyes at a distance. In fact, the records show that Sir John didn't have a daughter named Dorothy, but rather a sister by that name. And his sister married well, had several children and did not die a "raving maniac" in a far-off convent. There is, however, persuasive evidence that the ghost might be the unhappy spirit of a woman who was born to live in Samlesbury Hall but by a string of unfortunate circumstances ended up dying poor and starving in the streets.

Sir John's great granddaughter, Mary Southworth, was born in the very early years of the 17th century. Her father, another John, was the heir to the Samlesbury estates, but he died young and predeceased his father. As a result, Mary's older brother Thomas became the designated heir and claimed Samlesbury in 1617 when his grandfather died. Mary, instead of moving into the hall with her father, ended up being married at 13 or 14 to a poor Protestant cleric who lost his livelihood seven years into the marriage when people found out he had been counseling unwed mothers. He appealed to the Archbishop in 1633, and in one of his missives he begged for help, stating that his wife and son had succumbed to starvation and died in the streets. So poor Mary, born with a silver spoon in her mouth, died tragically with nothing to eat. In her misery, she may have yearned for the days of prosperity and what may have been if her father had inherited Samlesbury Hall. No doubt she visited the estate many times, so perhaps she still roves the grounds and the great halls, pining for a future that will never be.

# The White Witch of Rose Hall
## Montego Bay, Jamaica

Serial killer, slave torturer, temptress, tyrant. Jamaica's best-known ghost is not one to take lightly. Annie Palmer was her name and her evil doings finally did her in…or did they? The infamous "White Witch" lived during the 18th century on one of the largest sugar plantations on the island, and she not only abused and murdered three husbands and numerous slave lovers, but she also studied the ancient voodoo arts. Her powerful connection to the dark side could be the reason she still walks among us.

Admittedly, this story is hard to pin down—the facts tend to be a little malleable. I found several versions and not one was exactly the same, though they all agree that Annie essentially ran her plantation with a whip in one hand and a knife in the other. The diminutive French-born mistress of Rose Hall (she reportedly stood just four feet 11 inches tall) countered her short stature and gender with her own brand of violence in a time when lawlessness ruled in Jamaica.

When Annie arrived, Rose Hall plantation covered thousands of acres, ranging from the turquoise sea below to the green hills above. The Great House faces the sea so that its windows can open to refreshing tropical breezes, yet its thick stone walls are sturdy enough to resist hurricanes. Even today it stands as a monument to power and luxury. All the walls are white, in stark contrast to the dark mahogany of the floors, the library shelves and the furniture, all of which are from Rose Hall's own forest. The golden chains of the crystal chandeliers are wrapped in velvet to protect them from the salty sea air.

Annie came to the lush Caribbean island in 1790 to wed Rose Hall's owner, John Palmer. Some say she had already killed two previous husbands, while others say those men were yet to die at her hand. Unlucky for John, his beautiful wife got bored easily and preferred to give her wedding vows a helping hand by making sure death did allow her to part ways with her spouse. Perhaps she longed for the familiarity of her Parisian lifestyle with its outdoor cafes and sophisticated nightlife. Perhaps she was simply a sadist. How she killed him is part of the flexible legend—she either poisoned him or stabbed him. Then she ordered the slaves to dispose of the body. In those harsh days, when pirates still partied on Jamaica's white sands to celebrate their stolen booty, no one raised too much fuss when John Palmer disappeared. Annie continued her murderous romp unimpeded by the law.

Left alone to rule her personal kingdom, Annie took slaves as bedmates. However, she tired quickly of her lovers and one by one they were killed and buried in unmarked graves. Each morning, Annie pushed open the French doors to her second-floor balcony and stepped out to address the assembled slaves. She issued the day's orders, including who would join her in her bed that night. There was no choice—the men either died for refusing or died after submitting. To be chosen was to be doomed. All Annie's slaves lived in constant fear of their lives. Any resistance resulted in torture by the overseer in the plantation's dungeons. The only way out of Rose Hall was either to be sold or to be carried out feet first.

Annie carefully cultivated a powerful image of ruthlessness and magic powers. She knew women living alone were easy prey. That's probably why she delved so deeply into voodoo. Annie's slaves supposedly taught her everything they knew in order to keep themselves alive longer. As long as she needed them for their knowledge, they might be spared her whip or her whims of torture and death. Other stories say she actively studied voodoo under the tutelage of a Haitian princess. There are even rumors that she killed babies of her slaves to use the bones in voodoo rituals. Her prowess in both voodoo and other magic earned her the nickname "White Witch of Rose Hall," which still causes locals to shudder in fear.

As her power grew, her lust for blood intensified. (If it is true that she killed two husbands subsequent to John Palmer, one has to wonder where she met them because certainly any islander knew of her reputation.) But her dance of seduction and slaughter eventually was her undoing. Her last lover, according to some of the stories, was a slave engaged to the overseer's daughter. Although the overseer held the most powerful position of all the black people on the plantation, he had done nothing to stop the previous deaths for fear of his own life. This time, he could do nothing to prevent the inevitable—Annie apparently murdered the man on his first night in her bed rather than dallying with him for several nights. Motivated by his daughter's grief and his outrage at being so helpless, the overseer ignored orders to stay out of the house and entered Rose Hall. Now, some versions say he too practiced voodoo and entered a "to the death" match against Annie—which he survived just long enough to kill her and heave her body over the notorious balcony for the rest of the plantation's slaves to see.

The house on the hill was then abandoned. It was damaged during the slave rebellion of 1831, stripped of its mahogany door and magnificent furniture. The mansion fell into disrepair—no one would live there because Annie's ghost was said to still control the estate. One family purchased the property in 1905 and made preparations to move in, but thought better of it after a maid was somehow shoved out an upstairs window to her death. It wasn't until American John Rollins bought the estate in the mid-1960s and sank several million into restoring it that Rose Hall emerged from the cloud of fear and superstition to become an elegant hotel. Now it is more a museum, with a bar and restaurant. Tours are offered daily through the Rose Hall Great House, and many visitors claim to have had bizarre experiences. Judging by the number of photographs on display in the dungeons exhibiting strange phenomena, several people return home to find out they captured more than just a few memories in their photos. In particular, one mirror in Annie's bedroom is notorious for showing images of a woman who is not present when the photo is taken.

Furthermore, according to some witnesses, she can still be seen at night riding on Rose Hall's grounds wearing a green velvet dress, seated on a large black horse and flaying with her whip anyone in her way. Annie is said to manifest most frequently as a series of hurried footsteps heard walking through the main hall to the back entrance of the Great House. There are also reports of whispered voices in the dungeon, the sound of footsteps on the stairs and tapping on the walls. Some claim to hear the cries of the babies she murdered, as well as vintage music as if from some long ago cotillion. She may have also developed an affinity for electricity, delighting in turning lights on and off at random times.

After all this, it should be pointed out that it is possible the story of Annie is entirely myth, carried over from a popular story entitled "The White Witch of Rose Hall" by H.G. de Lisser. Margaret Morris, author of *Tour Jamaica*, goes even further in her research to state, "There is no historical evidence to substantiate this tale. The facts are that the Hon. John Palmer, Custos of St James, acquired Rosehall through marriage and built the great house. He was indeed the fourth husband of Rosehall's mistress, Mrs Rosa Palmer, but a memorial to her in St James Parish Church attests to her virtue and the fact that she died peacefully at age 72, predeceasing her husband. A subsequent Ann Palmer, wife of James Palmer, grandnephew of the Custos and heir to Rosehall, was also, research proves, a model wife."

All that has done nothing to stop the story from being perpetuated. As some storytellers will advise you, never let the facts get in the way of a good yarn. Over the years, various mediums have tried to contact Annie to verify her existence. One attempt in 1978 took place before a crowd of 8000 people. Psychics and spiritualists from around the world came to conjure up a link with Annie. For the most part, people were disappointed—Annie doesn't like to perform for a big group, it would seem. The only thing of note that took place was when Greek channeler Bambos claimed to have received a message from a stout lady who led him to her grave behind the house. There, buried inside a termite nest, he discovered an incense burner and voodoo doll believed to have belonged to Rose Hall's dead mistress.

Should you wish to visit, there is now a Ritz-Carlton hotel on the plantation property. The dungeon has been turned into a bar and souvenir shop. Apparently, the bar is a good place to start the tour as it serves up a special concoction called "The Witches Brew." The theory is that it makes you more attractive to Annie. As one recent ghost hunter wrote, "I can see why. After a couple of those, you would kiss a lamppost." On the other hand, maybe a sober head is a better way to meet this nefarious specter.

# 4

# Hotels & Inns

# England's Most Haunted House?

## WOTTON-UNDER-EDGE, GLOUCESTERSHIRE, ENGLAND

There's a bit of a quagmire I prefer to avoid when citing the status of a haunted place, giving it that vaunted title of "Most Haunted." I especially like to avoid this predicament in the UK, where it seems pretty much every place with an orb vies for the number one spot on the "ghost chart." You have to watch how the owners of various establishments phrase their claim to fame with tricky little extensions like "the most haunted pub *in the valley*" or "the most haunted inn *west of Wales.*" But an 11th-century home in the Gloucestershire village of Wotton-under-Edge, owned by a man named John Humphries, may be truly deserving of the "Most Haunted House" plaque for all of Britain. The Ancient Ram Inn is without a doubt the creepiest place for hundreds of miles around. After all, how many places boast not one but two lustful demons (an incubus *and* a succubus), countless orbs, a host of ghosts, a witch with a phantom cat, strange voices, oh, yes, and bone-numbing cold spots.

How can someone live in a house like this? Uneasily at best. John Humphries seems resigned to sharing his home with enough after-life creatures to populate a village though he admits he doesn't get much sleep. John's insomnia started on his very first night in the former working pub when he bought it in 1968. "The first night I slept in the house I was yanked out of bed by something or somebody which had grabbed hold of my ankles," he told the *Western Daily Press*. John swears he didn't know the house was haunted when he paid his £2600 for the musty inn that is believed to date back to 1145. "Over the years I have come to accept the ways of the house and you get used to staying out of certain rooms at certain times of the day and night."

It was John's daughters who apparently saw one of the inn's more unusual creatures quite often—a large, black, cat-like spirit they determined is an incubus. These evil lascivious male demons are said to sexually assault mortal women as they sleep and in the Middle Ages they were blamed for the birth of demons, witches and deformed children. According to one legend the incubus and his female counterpart, the succubus, were fallen angels. Whatever their origin, these spirits no doubt added to the feeling of unease felt by one priest who announced, "I'm not going in there, whatever you've got in there is very, very evil."

Some rooms are definitely worse than others. There's the Bishop's Room, for example. No fewer than eight people who have tried to spend a night in the room ended up spending time in the care of a priest who performed the rites of exorcism. So says John. Then there is the Witch's Room with its spectral cat, which supposedly uses the bed as a kitty litter, leaving a urine stain on the bedspread. I spoke with a paranormal investigator who says she and another member of her team bravely tucked in for the night on two occasions and were overwhelmed by the scary, strange things that happened, but never felt threatened or in danger.

Jo Holness of UK Paranormal visited The Ram in September 2003 with a colleague and again in March 2004. Her reports from both visits—shared with me for this book—highlight two rounds of non-stop nocturnal weirdness. They experienced flashing lights, plummeting temperatures, prickly pains and black shadowy shapes that literally crawled into bed with them. During a tour of the place on the first visit, Jo says she was drawn to the Witch's Room, and while John recounted the history of the room she saw a flash of bright light from under the stool at the dressing table. The room's curtains were drawn and it was "quite black" in the room at the time. Try as they might, neither Jo nor her companions could recreate the strange burst of light. Later during a silent vigil in both the Witch's Room and the Bishop's Room, Jo was "very aware of a black shape." She recalls, "I was sitting on the bed in the Witch's Room and could actually see a black shape moving. I couldn't make out any distinguishing features." The swarthy shape paced mere inches from where she sat. "I had the feeling you get when someone is checking you out, no malice or negativity, just of being observed." That same night Jo and her colleague switched to the Bishop's Room where they met another black shadowy being. Jo says it floated right above her face "like it was staring nose to nose at me." At one point the shadow nestled between Jo and her colleague, and just as she mentioned it he said he felt a cold draft blowing on his neck. Unlike other visitors who almost literally ran screaming from the room, Jo sensed no evil; however, it did make her uncomfortable. "I told it in no uncertain terms to back off from me and it did." Then she felt odd painful prickles starting in her feet and moving to various parts of her body. Other people who have slept in the room declare they have felt similar prickly sensations.

On a second visit to the Bishop's and Witch's rooms, Holness and Ray Matthews, another UK Paranormal investigator, attempted to contact the spirits with a Ouija board. They recorded their sessions with audiotape and video, and they also kept track of the temperature. Although the ghosts chose to ignore the question and answer session, it seems they did manage to communicate by causing the mercury to plummet more than 10°C or 18°F, in just over half an hour. When the investigators began to feel the initial freeze, Jo challenged the frosty wraith, "Can you drop the temperature more please?" In less than two minutes later the temperature dropped a few more degrees. During the session, Jo and Ray also heard strange tapping noises and thought there was movement near a closet. They left convinced the inn's spooky ambiance is more than just a product of overactive imaginations.

The Ram certainly acts as a magnet for paranormal groups trying to determine the exact nature of the spirits and perhaps find a reason for choosing this site. Neal Bardell of the National Paranormal Research Investigators still lists the Ancient Ram Inn as the place that produced the most paranormal activity in all his years of hunting ghosts. "I have seen with my own eyes a huge electric blue orb racing toward me then disappearing just before it hit me. Many of the group that was with us at the time also witnessed the sound of heavy furniture being moved around in the loft of the building," he stated during an interview. Then there's the Swindon-based bunch that operates as Paranormal Site Investigators (or PSI Ghostwatch). A dozen of their investigators spent the night and experienced the full gamut of paranormal nightlife, ranging from hearing unexplainable movement, to rattling door handles, moving objects, light anomalies and feeling something touch them. They also discovered, like many television crews wishing to document the mysterious events, that their equipment rapidly became non-functional as batteries drained and died. Jo Holness has a theory about that. She believes the Ram's spirits are ancient, not recent, and as such require large amounts of energy to sustain their presence on this plane. "Almost like a video replay being fed by new energies coming in, sort of like a battery pack recharging itself," she explained to me. "I went one time a couple of weeks after a TV crew had been filming and I noticed a distinctly negative feel to the place. John noticed it too. Then a few weeks later it was gone."

John Humphries agrees that much of the activity is related to the inn's earliest history. It is believed the crumbling stone structure was built above a pagan burial ground and was the site of black magic rituals and human sacrifice. A large hole in the middle of what used to be the bar floor is marked as a shrine to where the bones of a woman and child were found in a shallow grave.

There is a steady stream of visitors wanting to experience for themselves the creepy weirdness of the Ancient Ram Inn. Many have shared their observations with web sites that collect such stories. Stephen Barstow wrote of his haunted holiday to the BBC's online ghost story collection. He said that when he and his wife stayed at the Ram Inn in 1975, he froze in terror while in bed in the Bishop's Room (then the Berkeley Room) as a pair of glowing infant arms with wriggling fingers moved toward him in the dark. Other guests claim to have seen the ghost of a cavalier walk through the wall into their room. The ghost of a monk has been seen standing in front of the fireplace in one of the bedrooms. One small child told her parents, "I don't like that man sitting on my bed." Many guests feel the wrath of the ghost known as the Blue Lady, who seems to get her mettle up over messy beds. Dozens of people claim they have been pulled right off the bed or that their bedclothes are dumped on the floor. John Humphries has also seen the ghost of a woman in a long blue dress walk through one of his home's solid stone walls.

To return to the question of how one lives under such a robustly haunted roof, Jo Holness agrees it is a difficult life for John Humphries. "I think he's actually quite frightened to go in certain parts of the Ram. He avoids the bedroom areas unless he is taking people on a tour." She added, "I think he's quite a lonely man, and his fear and loneliness probably exacerbate what's going on because spirits feed on that kind of energy."

Regardless of your take on ghosts, the Ancient Ram Inn makes me think that a night in any of the rooms would only be welcome with the lights on.

# Cecil Plains Homestead
## Darling Downs, Queensland, Australia

The Shire of Millmerran is in the Darling Downs region of Queensland, 50 miles southwest of Toowoomba and 90 miles northeast of Goondiwindi. When Glennis and Daryl Philbey moved into an historic homestead there, they didn't expect to share their new house with ghosts. Bed-and-breakfasting tourists visiting Australia can now hope for glimpses of various ghostly personalities in the Cecil Plains Homestead. "Our ghosts! We have several," says Glennis Philbey. The ghosts have been seen at the oddest times. One is a lady wearing a high-necked dress and there are two men, one in a suit and the other more casually dressed. Footsteps are often heard in the house. The most memorable incident was when a ghostly figure rushed into the kitchen, touched Glennis on the shoulder and left *through* another door.

If you head into Cecil Plains, the homestead is at the eastern end of the town. Henry Stuart Russell founded the property in 1841, and Cecil Plains Station quickly became the focal point for life in the Australian outback. The station bred cattle and sheep, and developed into a thriving community. Glennis Philbey says it was also a hard life. "Many people died due to floods—being of English origin they knew little of water survival and farming accidents."

Henry named the homestead after his mother, Cecil Charlotte Pemberton. It started as a single slab cottage built on the western bank of the Condamine River, built by Henry and his brother Sydneham. Apparently Prussian explorer Ludwig Leichhardt often relaxed on the wide veranda with the two brothers, discussing his expedition plans. In 1859 Henry Russell sold the homestead to James Taylor and the Taylor family held it until 1916 when it became the property of the Crown to use for soldiers' settlement. Three years later, the land was thrown open for selection by soldiers returning from the Great War.

Jump ahead to the end of the 20th century. The building still stands in its original state with very little added or repaired. Daryl and Glennis purchased the property in 1999, now only 60 acres, considerably smaller than the station's original 200,000 acres. Glennis remembers when they moved in. "Many of the old photographs of the early owners lay on the floor on our arrival. It was at this time the first ghosts appeared, totally unhappy about the discard of their photos. The house was dark and cold. We opened every door leading onto the veranda which ran around the house, changed all the light bulbs from 25 watts to 100 watts and we felt the house sigh. As we added more warmth to the house the ghosts relaxed."

Among the first ghosts to appear was that of a woman; Glennis describes her as a tall, well-presented lady in 1860-80s-style clothing. The female phantom is thought to be the wife of the owner: Sarah Bolten. Then Glennis saw two gentlemen standing in what used to be the dining room, one in a dark suit, the other wearing casual clothes. The pair stood near an upright buffet, the only remaining piece of original furniture, apparently deep in conversation. Could they have been discussing the homestead's new owners?

The ghosts definitely relaxed once the Philbeys settled in. It wasn't long before Glennis and Daryl were greeted like family. "I was seated at the kitchen table one evening when the latched screen door in the kitchen suddenly opened. A man walked in, slapped me on the shoulder and walked out the other side screen door." In addition to getting welcoming pats, Glennis has heard her name called clearly on two occasions. She has seen a child playing up and down the back veranda with a bicycle. On a still night, she witnessed the clothesline turning around, whirling as if pushed by some playful spirit, which might have been easier to explain if it had not been weighted down with wet clothes. The Philbeys have also seen lights turn on in several rooms and found electric blankets turned on when they knew they had been carefully turned off. Having said all this, the ghosts are friendly and sharing the homestead with them is not a cause for concern.

Another ghost is rumored to roam the property. Some people have said that the phantom of the Prussian scientist and explorer who disappeared while making his second attempt to cross Australia still scouts about the homestead. Ludwig Leichhardt arrived in 1842 to study the country's rock and wildlife; he journeyed several times through the rough outback, including his most famous trip from Darling Downs to Port Essington, charting many of the unexplored rivers and mountains. He started most missions from Henry Russell's station, including the last ill-fated attempt to cross the country in 1848. Leichhardt may have been a brilliant explorer, but by all accounts he was a poor judge of character and not the best logistician. He hired a crew of misfits that often betrayed him or fought amongst themselves, and did not take enough provisions or horses. No one knows what happened to him or his crew of six men but they never returned. Nine extensive searches were conducted over the next century and aside from a few possible clues such as some bones and a coin, no one has ever solved the mystery of the vanishing expedition. Could it be that his crew mutinied and murdered him, leaving his body to be eaten by wild animals? Or were they all ambushed by Aborigines? Maybe they were caught in a sudden flood in Queensland's channel country and, unprepared for such an event, they drowned in the rushing waters.

However he met his end, some say Ludwig's spirit returned to the last place he considered home, unable to rest at peace. Glennis is not one of those who believe these stories. She hosts a festival every May in his honor, but feels that he is only present in the spirit of the event. "As for Ludwig's ghost, we portray him during the evening of Leichhardt's Festival. But as to him actually being one of my friendly ghosts, I doubt it very much," says Glennis. "We have a lot of fun on Saturday night imagining Leichhardt to be out and about, all in the course of adventure for those who came along for the festival."

# Ghosts, Not Gold, in the Alaskan Hotel

## JUNEAU, ALASKA, USA

It was rumors of gold that brought the first prospectors into the Alaskan Panhandle back in the late 1800s. Until then, the spruce-covered land was the domain of the Tlingit Indians who lived well off the rich salmon runs. It was a Tlingit guide who helped Joe Juneau and Richard Harris find gold on October 3, 1880 in the Silver Bow Basin, setting off a craze that would forever alter the landscape. The days of the gold rush are long over, and though the creeks no longer make someone an instant millionaire, cities like Juneau remain as monuments to the frenzy that drove men and women into the wilderness known as America's last frontier. The only way in is by boat or plane, and tourists will still venture to the southeastern part of Alaska in hopes of finding a nugget or two that was missed. Instead, they are more likely to find ghosts, leftover spirits from days that often saw as much death as they did good fortune.

In the craziness of those times, fortunes were made or lost in a day, men went mad with greed, and the unbridled nature of the surroundings seemed to be reflected in the goings-on after hours with plenty of drinking, gambling and girls to take what gold the men did find. Boomtowns like Juneau adapted to the increasing number of people arriving to try their luck with a gold pan, and hotels were built to accommodate the newcomers. In 1913 the Alaskan Hotel joined the growing number of inns that aimed to serve the public. It

*Some guests of the Alaskan Hotel have remained long after the gold rush days.*

still stands on South Franklin Street in the heart of Juneau's downtown area, the oldest continuously operating hotel in the city. And some of its guests date back to those early, early days of the gold rush: ghosts that like to give the paying guests a chill or a pat on the back, or an unexpected jolt by appearing in a mirror.

Like many of the businesses built to serve the gold rush era, the Alaskan Hotel doubled as a bordello. One of the ghost stories originates from the years when prostitutes had regular rooms in the local hotels. According to Alaska native and prolific author Ron Wendt, the ghost in the Alaskan Hotel is that of a woman who died at the hands of her husband within the building. The tale is tragic: the husband left to find his stake and make it rich, leaving his young wife behind. After three weeks, he had not returned and there was no word from him, and his wife thought he might not come back at all. Meanwhile, she ran out of money and resorted to prostitution to pay the bills. A few weeks later, the husband did return only to find his wife was now a working girl. Enraged, he murdered her in the hotel.

Now the woman's ghost haunts at least two rooms in the hotel. Staff and guests say there is something spooky about rooms 219 and 318. Cold chills, being touched and seeing a female figure sitting on the bed or reflected in the mirror are some of the experiences people have reported. A number of guests just can't take it and ask to be moved to another room. Jeff Belanger, who has written his own book about the world's most haunted places, interviewed a front desk clerk who had heard all the stories but not seen anything himself. Did he disbelieve the ghost tales? No, because as he put it, "parts of the hotel just don't feel right."

Straight-shooting manager Scott Fry told me that he has lost count of his years at the Alaskan, though he reckons the number is around 12 or 15. He started out as a doorman, then worked as the night auditor and did pretty much everything in between that and being "the next best thing to the owner." In all those years, he has not seen any ghosts. On the other hand, he states in a well-rehearsed patter that he is a firm agnostic and to him "seeing is believing." As he succinctly put it, "I'm not prone to seeing them." But he has heard an amazing number of stories from people who swear they saw something supernatural, and he's willing to share those tales. He says the most haunted room is 312, and that pretty much all the rooms at the back of the hotel in the 18s or 19s where the working girls used to have their rooms are the most active. But room 312 is the one that people complain about the most as being haunted. "That's the room that we believe the woman died in," says Scott. "Her name is Alison." Recently, a friend and former front desk clerk at the hotel told Scott of an experience he had one night when a guest phoned down from room 312 in some distress asking for help. The clerk went up and knocked on the door, fearing he might encounter some sort of domestic dispute. A frightened woman's voice called out that she couldn't answer the door, he would have to open it himself. When the clerk entered, he saw the woman standing over in the corner wrapped in a bed sheet, shaking and pointing at the bathroom, saying, "He's in there." Now very worried, the clerk knocked on the door and called to the person inside to come out. When no one answered, he opened the door to find an empty room. The terrified woman then told him there was no man, but that she'd seen a ghost move through her room and into the bathroom.

After many shifts on night audit, Scott says if he was going to see a phantom, it would be then. "The whole hotel is asleep. The whole town is asleep. You're the only one awake. But there are a lot of mirrors in this place. You could easily convince yourself you'd seen something out of the corner of your eye and it would just be you moving." Does he think the stories are just figments of creative imaginations? "Some people do come here asking if we have ghosts," he says, "so maybe they expect to see something. But people come from all over—from Bangor, Maine to Florida—and without knowing anything, they say they've seen a ghost."

A former guest of the hotel had one of the strangest experiences in the ladies' washroom. No ghost, but a bit of a time slip. She walked in to use the facilities and found a lovely antique washroom with the old-style sinks and amenities. On her second trip to the loo, the room was modern. Confused, the woman asked someone where the old bathroom had gone, but no one knew what she was talking about. The newer bathroom had been in place for years.

Is Alison's ghost perpetually checked into room 312? Do other spirits camp out in the hotel's older section? In the words of Scott Fry, "Some people say so."

# The Lady in Red
## VANCOUVER, BRITISH COLUMBIA

It stands to reason that an elegant hotel would have an upper-class wraith. And the opulent and historic Hotel Vancouver in downtown Vancouver, British Columbia, is no exception to that theory. The ghost of a lady wearing either a red cape or long red ball gown has been seen gliding about the 14th floor and riding in the elevators. Though there have been several sightings, hotel staff are reluctant to draw attention to their phantom. "For as many people as it intrigues, it also puts people off," says Jill Killeen, who manages the hotel's public relations.

William Cornelius Van Horne began work on the Hotel Vancouver in 1912 for the Canadian Pacific Railway. Even then, its magnificence surpassed most other buildings; it towered over neighboring structures, its copper roof glinting in the sunlight. It officially opened amid much fanfare, including the presence of King George VI and Queen Elizabeth, in 1939. Even though the copper roof has since turned green, it is still one of Vancouver's finest buildings, with its imposing towers, turrets and gargoyles. The interior is reminiscent of a refined, chic French chateau with marble, mirrors, sculptures, and mahogany and maple furnishings.

The ghost is believed to date from those early days when the hotel first opened. In fact, Jill Killeen says there may be a whole family of phantoms. When the ghost is seen, people refer to her wearing a fancy red period ball gown or floor-length cape. It is believed that the woman, her husband and daughter attended functions such as gala dances and formal teas at the hotel. That would explain the red cape. The Lady in Red has been seen both alone and with her husband and daughter in tow. And nearly all sightings are up on the 14th floor, either in the elevator or in the lobby area, though there have been a couple of notable exceptions. "There is a certainly a different feel to the 14th floor," says Killeen. "It's the floor with the royal parlor and some of the larger suites. It has a different design, the walls are covered in dark wood paneling—it just has a distinctly different feel. It's hard to explain."

At the end of 1995 and the beginning of the following year, there was a lot of activity at the hotel because renovation work was underway. During that time, there seemed to be a spike of supernatural activity as well. Guests and staff reported several sightings of the Lady in Red and her family.

One of the hotel housemen was up on the 14th floor late at night making his rounds when the elevator door opened. There was a woman, man and child standing there, but they didn't get off. The houseman saw that the woman was wearing a red cape. The elevator doors closed, and he suddenly realized the three passengers were in an elevator shaft that had no elevator in it! Jill Killeen explained that when the hotel was built, the engineers constructed eight shafts but only six were ever made operational. And on all the other floors, there are only six elevator doors, but on the 14th floor, all eight doors had already been installed before the decision was made to go with only six working elevators. On top of that, the doors that opened to reveal the ghostly trio are bolted shut. "The houseman was sufficiently spooked," says Killeen.

*The Lady in Red is often seen on her way back from a party in the hotel's elegant ballroom.*

Then there's the story of the cameraman who worked, ironically, on *The X-Files*, the popular television series about the paranormal. He was staying on the 14th floor and was up late one night. The cameraman apparently looked out his window and could make out the massive gargoyles that were level with the 14th floor. But what he could also see was the terrifying sight of a woman in red hovering next to one of the prominent gargoyles. "And that sufficiently frightened him," says Killeen, summing up his story.

Killeen says she has heard that ghosts don't necessarily haunt where they died, but haunt where they were happiest. "Now that's not a PR thing. With our ghost, we have only ever had sightings, no interaction." She said there is another story of a young Japanese couple who went to check into their room, but when they unlocked the door they saw a lady in a red cape sitting on the end of the bed. Apologizing profusely, they closed the door and went down to the front desk to say they must have been given the wrong key, as their room was occupied. The front desk assured them that they had not entered the wrong room and that the room was vacant; so, the couple returned to the room with someone from the front desk and no one was there. But the couple insisted they had seen a woman wearing red.

The hotel was always a focal point for Vancouver's grand balls and galas, and it still is a major site for formal functions in the city. There have not been any sightings of the Lady in Red that Jill knew of in the last four or five years, but the theory that the hotel staff feel is most plausible is that their crimson-loving entity has been most often seen on her way back from a party. Perhaps she found life on the other side to be less entertaining than she had hoped, and prefers the company of the hotel's posh revelers. Or it may well be that her spirit has indeed moved on, but—as some paranormal experts believe—her psychic energy was so strong while she was alive that she left behind an imprint that is still occasionally visible. So, should you attend a function at the sumptuous hotel ballroom, watch for visitations from an uninvited, elegant and otherworldly guest.

# Monte Cristo Homestead
## JUNEE, NEW SOUTH WALES,
### AUSTRALIA

Perched high on a hill overlooking the peaceful New South Wales town of Junee, Monte Cristo looms like a tall, creepy shadow, stretched into a larger-than-life version of itself by the dozens of stories of ghosts within. It is known far and wide as Australia's "most haunted house." With so much media hype nowadays—pumped up by television shows that would like viewers to believe they have been let in on spooky secrets—it can be hard to know if that title is deserved or pure invention to draw in ratings. However, based on research by some reputable paranormal organizations and the stories told by the family that has lived in Monte Cristo since 1963, there is little doubt the two-story mansion is very, very haunted.

Reg Ryan, his wife Olive and their three children moved into the home called Monte Cristo on June 3, 1963. They were the first to live in it after the original owners vacated in 1948, leaving it to the mercy of vandals and looters. The Ryans took it over despite its deplorable conditions, prepared to restore the manor to its former glory. In its heyday, the graceful Victorian homestead belonged to Christopher William Crawley and his wife Elizabeth. Crawley was a farmer who made some shrewd land purchases and built a hotel near what would become the main railway line through town. His investments and visionary thinking made him a rich man. With his newfound wealth, Crawley built the sprawling

*The beautifully renovated Monte Cristo*

home atop the area's only real hill in order to enjoy the view. Unfortunately, an infected boil on Mr. Crawley's neck cut short his enjoyment—he died at Monte Cristo in 1910 at age 69. His widow, Elizabeth, lived out the rest of her life in the house. She became quite religious and turned part of the upper floor into her own private chapel. With a personal sanctuary on site, there didn't seem to be any need to leave—in the 23 years that Elizabeth lived alone on the hill she only left her home twice. She died in 1933 at age 92 from a ruptured appendix. Apparently, she didn't leave her home then either.

This brings us back to the Ryan family and Reg Ryan who spied the abandoned house for sale in 1955. For a tailor from Wagga Wagga, it was a lot of money and seemed insane given the dilapidated state of the structure. All the windows were broken, doors were smashed off their frames, walls had been damaged, and even the main staircase had been cut in two. But for Reg Ryan, this house spoke to him. From the first moment that he saw it, he says he knew he would own it. "The day I saw it, my life completely changed," he told me. It took him eight years to work out the deal, and from the first days there, he and his family discovered its secrets. The spirits of former owners and residents hadn't abandoned Monte Cristo at all; they just kept to themselves until the new owners took over. Then they let the Ryans know they had company.

The Ryans had only been installed in the house for three days when the first indication of something strange occurred. Reg and Olive had driven into town on a very foggy night to pick up supplies and when they returned they were stunned to see their home lit up like a Christmas tree. Light poured from within, filling every window and doorway, creating a huge beacon in the thick mist. On the Monte Cristo web site, which includes Reg's account of their various ghostly encounters, he says that he stopped the car and they both stared at this unbelievable phenomenon. His wife thought it might be burglars, but Reg knew that wasn't possible because unless they brought their own battery packs and handheld lights, there wasn't any electricity hooked up and the only source of light was an unlit kerosene lamp. They couldn't even convince themselves that it was a reflection from their car's high beams, because the lights in the house went out as they drove through the gateway and up the driveway. "This was the first of many strange, puzzling and sometimes frightening experiences that have occurred over the intervening years we have not found answers for," says Reg. Since then, the Ryans discovered several areas of the house that are haunted. Some of the spirits are obvious. Others remain a mystery.

Mrs. Crawley, said to rule her manor with an iron fist, still dominates her spiritual world. Of all the ghosts, she is the one people notice most often. She has been known to order visitors out of the dining room and has created a distinctly unwelcoming energy in the room that was her chapel. Reg Ryan notes that of the people who visit the house—and hundreds do every year—it is mainly young girls who experience Mrs. Crawley's negative energy. In 1996 Reg found a girl outside the house wandering about, lost from her tour group. She told him that as she was about to enter the house, an older woman in period clothing confronted her and shouted at her "to get out of her house." No one else in the house at the time matched the unwelcoming woman's description—Reg knows that it was the former matriarch staking out her spiritual turf. Olive Ryan told me that Mrs. Crawley doesn't like her much either. Olive says, "She's always telling me to move out. It's a bit weird, but I intend to live out the rest of my life here so there's not much she can do about it."

Another woman told the Ryans that she witnessed Elizabeth after one of the annual fancy dress balls, which are thrown every fall. As the woman drove away, she stopped to look at the house lit up at night. While she gazed on Monte Cristo, a woman in an old-fashioned dress walked the length of the second-floor balcony. At first the woman thought it was just one of the guests in costume, until she passed the French doors. The lights from the window shone right through the strolling figure. Reg Ryan has heard the clear tap of a woman's high heels walking along the balcony and so has his family. There are times when they still hear footsteps even

*People have encountered floating lights, doors that close and eerie sounds inside the Monte Cristo.*

though the area is now carpeted. There is more to the story of Mrs. Crawley, though. Reg and Olive explained to me that she was part Aboriginal and after her husband's death, she was ostracized by the community. "The marriage was not acceptable at the time," says Reg. Not only that, her own children refused to come to see her. "It was a very lonely 23 years," muses Olive. Could the sorrow of those years continue to hold Elizabeth Crawley to this plane?

Mr. Crawley's ghost also keeps up appearances at his earthly home. A more benign presence, he tends to observe the people coming to tour through his home rather than try to prevent them from visiting. A little boy recently spent most of the tour looking behind him rather than paying attention to the various rooms. No one thought anything of it, until he asked his mother in the car why the man in a brown suit with a gray beard had followed them around.

The Ryans have a long list of other weird sightings and strange occurrences, both inside and outside the house. Guests have been overcome by bizarre asthma attacks, fainting spells, crying jags and even a sense of being possessed. The Ryan children used to see a man's face floating outside their bedroom window, and more recently a relative who stayed overnight claims to have seen a white floating figure move about the same room before floating through the closed window. The staircase, according to Reg, "often causes problems, especially with children." There was a tragic death on the staircase when one of the Crawleys' daughters fell down the stairs and was fatally injured. The girl was being carried by her nanny at the time. The nanny claimed the child was pushed from her arms by some invisible force. Whether her story is true doesn't change the odd goings-on in this area of Monte Cristo. One woman and her daughter taking the tour found they could not climb the staircase because an unseen force prevented them from moving. Reg Ryan isn't sure that the death of the child is connected to the paranormal activity on or near the stairs, though it certainly seems likely.

In fact, there is a trio of ghostly children in the house. Of the Crawley's ten children, only seven survived into adulthood. In addition to the staircase death, one girl died after her dress caught fire while standing near the fireplace. She ran outside as her dress flamed around her, and burned to death. A Crawley boy also died, but his cause of death is a mystery. Mediums who visit the house claim to see the walls of one room covered in blood and feel certain he was murdered, but there is no record of a violent death in the house. Reg continues to investigate but told me he hasn't been able to find the truth behind the boy's death. His ghost is seen fairly frequently. Reg told me that children who come to visit the house often ask their parents "Why wouldn't those other children talk to us?" A young boy in a 19th-century sailor suit has been seen sitting in a tree in one of the gardens, and he is sometimes accompanied by a girl in a similar outfit. In the early 1990s, one local mother told the Ryans that her children saw the boy in the garden and called out for him to join them, but he vanished before their eyes.

Recently, a couple staying in one of the rooms above the old homestead awoke to see an entire Crawley family of apparitions floating in their room. "There was a man, woman, boy and girl," Reg related to me. As with most of these sightings, when the people saw portraits of the original owners, the identity of the apparitions is confirmed. The list of stories goes on and on. There are incidents in most of the outbuildings, including the stables and the coach house. People have encountered floating lights, doors that close and eerie sounds.

Monte Cristo no longer hovers above Junee as a derelict, but gleams from the hard work and elbow grease that the Ryan family put into restoration. The house is filled with antiques and art and closely resembles the days when Christopher and Elizabeth Crawley lived there. Reg Ryan will tell you he still cannot resist the pull of this house. "I don't want to leave. I'm going to be the next ghost," he says with a laugh. He is sure that something supernatural guided him to be guardian and caretaker of the homestead. His sense is that the spirits, which he feels quite often, especially in the drawing room, approve of him. "They were a bit hectic when we first came, but they've calmed down now." Good thing, after nearly 42 years. Olive, however still has her troubles.

"My wife is not comfortable here, and if anything happens to me, she'll move right away. Good of her to keep me company all these years. It must be love."

The Ryans' children are grown, have moved away and have families of their own. With the extra space, the Ryans now operate a bed-and-breakfast that includes a ghost tour. If you are brave enough, give them a call and book yourself a room.

# Phantom in Franschhoek
## FRANSCHHOEK, SOUTH AFRICA

Picturesque, lush, charming. Those adjectives apply to the Old World town of Franschhoek, on South Africa's Western Cape in the heart of the Winelands. You could also use *haunted*—if on your way through you happen to stay at one of the local guest houses. East, formerly Le Ballon Rouge, houses at least one ghost that the current owners and staff run into with eerie frequency. You too might be met by greetings of "good evening" from the invisible house guest.

Lesley Dennis and her husband Kevin bought East in late 2002, happy to be owners of the Victorian-style guest house and restaurant. The fairy-tale village of Franschhoek is not only stunningly scenic, but also renowned as the food and wine capital of the Cape. The town's name literally means "French corner," and it is in this valley that many Huguenots of France sought refuge from religious persecution in the 17th century after King Louis XIV revoked the Edict of Nantes. French influence permeates the region. Its abundance of wineries and top-quality cuisine is what drew Lesley and her husband to become the proprietors of East. Little did they know that they were about to become hosts to a ghost.

"We have had a few experiences of our ghost," Lesley told me. "There is an old lady who walks our corridor between the kitchen and the back office, past the bar area." One evening at about 8 PM, Lesley swears she heard a woman's voice wish her "Good evening." She looked around to see who was speaking but there was no one else in the room. "It was a very definite 'good evening' but no one was there!"

Lesley *might* have convinced herself that she was hearing things if both her husband and their barman, Chris Norris, had not also heard voices and footsteps when the place was empty. Kevin heard a woman's voice and the tread of footsteps in the bar area while he was working in the office. When he investigated, he found himself alone. And Chris stopped in to see Lesley one evening while she toiled in the office, asking if she had said something. "I said no," she recalls, "but I had just heard a lady's voice speaking to him! There was only the two of us in the building."

In fact, before knowing East is haunted, Chris had a particularly strange experience that Lesley witnessed. He had only been on staff for a few weeks, and was leaning over the reception desk to speak to Lesley while she sat in the office. He suddenly shuddered and said that he felt as if "someone had walked over his grave." He told Lesley he went "all cold inside." Lesley then confessed that Chris stood directly in the path of the ghostly woman who walks the corridor. That news distressed him, and he moved quickly out of the way saying the experience left him feeling very odd.

Other odd things happen. Lights studiously turned off the night before burn brightly when Lesley and Kevin arrive in the morning. "Kevin was with me the evening we put the lights out in the front lounge area, as we both double-checked they were off before we left, but then in the morning we were both witness to the fact that the lights were on," says Lesley.

In early September 2004, a large picture that had been hanging for years in the bar area inexplicably fell off its hook in the middle of the night, but did not set the alarm off. Lesley says that just as odd is that two items fell off the piano, which sits under the picture, but a tall glass candle holder did not move.

All very interesting experiences, no question. But for Lesley, what raised all this to another level was the day one of her guests came forward saying he discerned a ghostly presence in his room. "A guest staying in bedroom 5 asked if we had a ghost here," she told me. The guest then revealed "he had felt someone standing by his bed the night before, and there was a definite presence in the room." Lying in the dark, the man opened his eyes and could make out the shape of a woman. He also heard her speak, but when he turned on the light no one was there. That incident prompted Lesley to register East on the International Ghost Hunters Society web site, which is how I found them.

Who is the mystery phantom? Apparently, it is the ghost of the original owner. Built in 1908, the homestead belonged to one family and then was converted into two houses. Just prior to the conversion, the first owner—an elderly woman—died in her bed. Her death occurred in what are now guest bedrooms 5 and 6 at East.

Lesley Dennis met one of the previous owners of the house who told her they too had experiences of the "lady" walking the corridor. As for the recent spate of weird visits, Lesley says, "She does not scare me. But we are doing a lot of changes to the business right now, and I think she has probably been unsettled!"

# Yun Shan Fan Dian Hotel
## CHENGDE, CHINA

The small city of Chengde in the craggy mountains north of Beijing used to shelter Qing Dynasty notables, including the Empress Dowager Cixi, from Beijing's sweltering summer heat. Tourists still flock to Chengde to escape Beijing during the hot summer months, taking in the scenery, the temples and the historic Imperial Summer Villa. Among the decent hotels at which to stay is the 220-room Yun Shan Fan Dian on Nan Yuan Road overlooking the Yangtze River. Guests there may find that the empress still spends time overlooking her former gardens; the ghost of a woman wearing the ancient robes of an empress has been seen both inside the hotel and on one of the hotel's upper balconies.

Cixi, whose given name is somewhat of a mystery, rose to power in the tumultuous times of the 19th century. From very humble roots as daughter of a low-ranking government official, she became a lady in waiting at the Forbidden Palace and soon became the Emperor Xianfeng's concubine. Before long, she gave the emperor his only son. Upon his deathbed, Xianfeng arranged that his five-year-old son Tongzhi should succeed him, and that his wife and his mistress should take the titles Ci'an (Empress Mother) and Cixi (Empress Dowager) respectively. Though Tongzhi ascended the throne, in truth the real power lay with the young emperor's mother. No woman in China could officially hold office as an emperor, so the ambitious Cixi had to rule through her son to push through her policies. She was quite literally the woman behind the man. The emperor sat in

*Does the Empress Dowager wander the halls of the Chengde hotel out of boredom in the afterlife?*

front of a golden screen in his meetings with nobles and officials, while the two empresses Cixi and Ci'an sat behind the curtain, listening to the reports and making state decisions. However, it soon became quite apparent that Cixi made most of the decisions, becoming known as clever and controlling. Then Ci'an died suddenly and it was rumored that Cixi had poisoned her. As time went on, the Empress Dowager lost interest in ruling and became more consumed by narcissistic pleasures such as clothes and jewelry. She spent money earmarked for the Chinese navy to redo the gardens at her summer palace. Cixi ruled for more than 40 years, and many believe her pursuit of pleasure was almost the undoing of the Qing Empire, which collapsed in 1912 when revolutionaries overthrew the dynasty to establish the Chinese Republic. She died in 1908, though it has been suggested that her indomitable spirit still seeks out the cooler breezes of Chengde.

On the eighth floor of the Yun Shan Fan Dian Hotel, witnesses claim to have seen a woman walking at the end of the hall dressed in the distinctive robes of an empress. The woman is also seen standing on the balcony of the same floor, peering down on people below. She is sometimes surrounded by the ghosts of her servants. Who is this stately specter? Is it Cixi, displaced but still connected to Chengde? Or could it be Ci'an, the murdered empress, watching the goings-on at the Imperial Summer Palace from a safe distance?

# 5

# Odd Places

# Cricket, Anyone?
## PIETERMARITZBURG,
## KwaZulu-Natal, South Africa

This little story is short but I found it compelling because it is unlike most other ghost tales I come across. It stands out because of the location and the unlikely daytime haunting. A cricket pitch in the very beautiful Alexandra Park in the South African city of Pietermaritzburg is home to a ghostly game, an annual phantom pilgrimage.

Should it happen that you visit the park on a hot summer afternoon and notice a thick fog rolling up from the Duzi River, my advice is don't head for home. Instead, as the fog obliterates the cricket pavilion from sight, stay put and keep quiet. There's a good chance you will hear the sounds of a spectral set of "ends" as voices call out instructions or encouragement to invisible players.

According to some reports, people have heard what must be the umpire's voice calling "No ball" or "End of the over." Men's voices call to their teammates, saying "Run!" or "Stay!" and there is even a refined "Well played" called when a phantom player does well. From the fog-covered grandstand, witnesses say they have heard one woman clapping her hands and excitedly exclaiming "Bravo! Well done!"

Of course, if you remain until the fog lifts you will be alone on the cricket pitch. The grandstand will be empty and no players or umpires will be gathering up their equipment. The game dissolves with the dissipating fog. Who are these players that return for their annual match? And who is the lone woman in the Pavilion?

# Ghost Mountain
## KwaZulu-Natal, South Africa

*It is a great and strange Mountain. It is haunted also and named the Ghost Mountain, and on top of it is a grey peak rudely shaped like the head of an old woman.*
—Rider Haggard's *Nada the Lily*

The eerie glow of nighttime flames dots the slopes of KwaZulu-Natal's imposing mountain, but in the bright light of day no signs of burning exist. This is the legend of Ghost Mountain. The mountain is part of the Ubombo range, which stretches northwards for 375 miles and once formed the shores of a primordial sea. Towering over the small village of Mkuze, the double peaks of Gaza and Tshaneni are impressive craggy stakes to mark an ancient royal Zulu burial ground and the home of many unsettled spirits.

Zulu legend focuses mainly on Tshaneni—"the place of the small stone"—where people say the side of the mountain lights up at night with the fires of the dead. There is no pattern to the sighting of strange flickering; it happens irregularly, yet often enough that some local residents still take precautions against evil spirits when walking out on the mountain at night. Weird noises and peculiar calls have also been heard. When you look into the mountain's history, as author Rider Haggard did, it is easy to see why the slope that was at one time a battlefield full of bones is haunted nowadays.

Haggard knew the area well. He explored it extensively during the years when he worked at the nearby Ubombo courthouse. That was when Zululand was still a British

Protectorate and he was in colonial service. Haggard wandered around the base of the mountain many times, digging into both its rocky ground and its grim history. He knew the local people refused to join him on his walks, but he could never get them to articulate why except to say only that the steep land was too frightening. In 1892 Haggard wrote in his book *Nada the Lily* that on one of his trips around Ghost Mountain, "we came across the ruins of a kraal and in it lay the bones of many men." Among the skeletons were weapons and shields made from ox hide—these were the remains of warriors who died in one of the many hillside slaughters that occurred on Ghost Mountain.

This mountain is shrouded in death and secrecy. First there is the history of the Ndwandwe tribe whose leaders, members of the Gaza family, lived in the somber shadow of the impressive peaks and buried their chiefs in a secret cave somewhere high up on the mountain. The Gaza family was conquered by the Shaka and was driven out of the area in 1819. They fled to Mozambique where their leader Shoshangane formed the Shanganes tribe. Leaving their homeland did not mean abandoning their tradition of burying their chiefs on the mountain—it just meant they had to be much sneakier in doing it. Members of tribe wrapped the deceased body along with any personal possessions in the skin of a black bull. Then family members carried the mummified remains all the way back to Ghost Mountain. They traveled strictly under cover of dark to avoid being caught by the Zulus. To this day the cave remains a secret burial ground because no one has been able to locate it. Could it be that the spirits of the dead Ndwandwe chiefs meet on the mountain to mourn the loss of their homeland?

More violent and more recent is the bloody battle between two chieftains who ruled after the Anglo-Zulu wars in 1879. Zululand was at the time still under British control when Sir Garnet Wolseley split it into 13 states, which resulted in chaos and massive civil unrest as the separate areas fought among themselves for more land. Two of the most aggressive and powerful rivals were Sibebu, head of the Mandlakazi faction of the Zulu nation, and Dinizulu, son of deposed Zulu king Cetshwayo. The two men were determined to rule the Zulus and pulled out all the stops to see they won. Initially it appeared Sibebu would win; a superior tactician, he tipped the scales in his favor after emerging victorious from several bloody skirmishes. However, Dinizulu's hunger for power drove him to forge alliances with 800 white frontiersmen—many of them Boers. The white mercenaries agreed to fight alongside Dinizulu's men in exchange for farmland. On June 5, 1884, in what came to be known as the Battle of Ghost Mountain, Dinizulu invaded Sibebu's territory. He confronted the leader and his army in a jagged gorge at the base of the mountain, and with the aid of the frontiersmen's rifles, mowed down the majority of Sibebu's talented but under-equipped warriors. After the slaughter, piles of corpses littered the mountain. Years later, in 1920, visitors such as Colonel Denys Reitz noted in one of his books that heaps of bones still lay strewn around the hillside.

Flash-forward to present day and farmer Larry Stephens now grows cotton on the land that once ran red with blood. He hasn't seen any ghosts, doesn't believe in ghosts and doesn't particularly like talk of ghosts. He prefers to believe the supposition by a visiting scientist that the bizarre lights might be from the phosphorescent glow of the bones.

Apparently, under the right conditions, that is possible. But other people who live in sight of Ghost Mountain still respect the dead spirits they believe haunt the land. Sipho Twala lives in Mkuze and will not leave his home at night without matches in his hair and salt in his palms—a concoction taught to him by his grandfather to ward off evil spirits. Local guide Thokozani Mdluli believes the strange sounds heard by passersby are not of this world. "Many died here," he told author Stephen Coan. "Later when noises were heard people said [these were] the voices of the people who died here."

Do the ghosts of dead Zulu warriors still light the fires of war, planning for the next attack? Perhaps they guard the land now as vigilantly as they did hundreds of years ago, unaware that their services are no longer required.

# Ghost Planes of Derbyshire
## SHEFFIELD, SOUTH YORKSHIRE, ENGLAND

The rugged rocky outcrops of Northern England's Sheffield Peaks are extremely beautiful—the Himalayas or the Rockies they are not. They are high enough, however, to have claimed the lives of more than 300 people during World War II because 50 low-flying aircraft somehow crashed into the South Yorkshire hills. Nowadays, some of those very planes are often seen by local residents, skimming the sky silently on a ghostly voyage with no end. Sightings of phantom airmen have also been reported, though less frequently than the ghost planes.

The most commonly seen ghost planes involve air disasters that happened toward the end of the war. In May 1945 a Royal Canadian Air Force Lancaster bomber crashed at an area called James' Thorn, and two months later a USAF Dakota crashed at the nearby Shelf Moor. Thirteen airmen died in the two accidents. In November 1948, shortly after the war, a US Superfortress carrying Captain Landon P. Tanner and his crew hit the ground, killing everyone on board.

As you might expect, most of the sightings happen near where the planes went down, by the Derwent and Ladybower Reservoirs, which lay south of the Howden Moors, the largest of the Peak District's many moors. During the 1980s, a group of aircraft archeologists touring the area near James' Thorn climbed up 2000 feet for a better view from the shelf of where the American plane piloted by Captain Tanner crashed. Crash investigator Gerald Scarratt outlined the history of the accident and as he spoke members of the group saw a man wearing flying gear standing behind him. They asked who he was and when Mr. Scarratt turned to look, the man disappeared. Many believe they saw the ghost of Captain Tanner.

Retired postman Tony Ingle went for a walk with his eight-year-old retriever Ben on a spring day in 1995 and got an unexpected shock. As they ambled in the May sunshine, Tony looked up when the sun's warmth suddenly vanished behind a cloud. What Tony saw brought him to a standstill. There was no cloud. Instead, a large plane passed only 50 feet above his head, banking to the left. Tony told one reporter that he could see the plane was in trouble. The old military aircraft careened toward the ground and disappeared behind a hedge. Tony sprinted up the lane expecting to see flames and smoke pouring from the plane wreckage but as he reached a place where he could see into the nearby field, there were only animals grazing peacefully, and no sign of the plane anywhere. Then it dawned on Tony that he had seen the plane's propellers moving but hadn't heard any sound. The silence struck him as very eerie. A few days later, he asked a researcher from the *Sheffield Journal* about plane crashes in the area and was told that in 1945 an American Dakota crashed in a dense fog about 50 yards from where Tony Ingle had been standing. Tony's dog Ben apparently refuses to go near the field; Tony himself claims to not believe in ghosts—though he has no explanation for what he saw and says he is disturbed by the experience.

Certainly the most memorable event happened on a cold, clear night in 1997 when not one but dozens of people, outside to look for the comet Hale-Bopp, witnessed a propeller-driven plane struggle to stay airborne as it flew by.

The aircraft then appeared to crash in Howden Moors, northwest of Sheffield. Just after 10 PM, two farmers living near Bolsterstone were the first to call the police and ask if they had any reports of an aircraft crashing. Within 15 minutes the operations room at Ecclesfield police station was inundated with calls from witnesses who saw a plane go down, along with a huge flash and plumes of smoke. Some claimed to see a bright orange glow light up the night sky, and they were quite clear it was not the comet. Others heard a loud crash. In Derbyshire and South Yorkshire the police stations received more calls from reliable witnesses; by 10:30 PM the local fire and rescue teams were on full alert for what sounded like an aircraft disaster.

A large-scale search and rescue began before midnight with a police helicopter and a Sea King helicopter scouring the area using searchlights and high-tech thermal imaging equipment to hunt for any signs of wreckage or fire. Meanwhile, the military and civilian air controllers reported they had not lost any planes in the region. Hospitals pulled in extra staff in case of casualties while rescue teams from every surrounding district raced toward the moors. However, no crash sight was spotted in the aerial search, so the emergency workers cooled their heels at a local inn and the mountain rescue teams were deployed. Nearly 150 volunteers set out on foot, some with dog teams, to hunt through more than 50 square miles of some of England's most inhospitable territory.

As dawn broke, the *Sheffield Star* ran with the search as one of the lead stories for Wednesday, March 25, 1997. "Emergency services from four counties were today involved in a massive operation to solve an *X-Files*-style air crash riddle in South Yorkshire." The newspaper went on to report,

"The operation was launched after a suspected air crash and explosion were reported on Peak District moorland near Sheffield. Police treated the reports seriously because callers reporting the incident were so specific—even though air traffic authorities had no official reports of missing aircraft."

Despite dozens of detailed reports of a low-flying aircraft, a massive explosion and plumes of smoke, searchers found not one single bit of crumpled metal. After 15 hours of unsuccessful combing through the moors, emergency officials called off the search. Mountain rescue coordinator Mike France reported, "There was no scouring to the moor, there were no bits of wreckage. There was no oil traces on the reservoirs." He found the whole incident confusing and so did police, who left the incident officially "unexplained." One police statement allowed that there might be something to local tales about ghost planes in the area. "No explanation was ever found and we remain open-minded about what was behind the sightings."

Was it a ghost plane? Could it have been a UFO, as many people suggest? Or was it, as some investigators insist, a covert military exercise? After all these years, and dozens of investigations, there are still no clear answers. So, did hundreds of people see the same air-borne apparition at the same time? Perhaps we'll never know. One thing is certain— the mysterious moors of Sheffield aren't telling.

# Pluckley's Many Phantoms
## PLUCKLEY, KENT, ENGLAND

In 1998 *Guinness World Records* acknowledged the small village of Pluckley as the most haunted village in England. That's quite a feat for a place with barely 1000 people noted on the population sign. If the tales are true, there is roughly one ghost for every 62.5 people living in Kent's quaint community. From the ghostly coach and horses to the monk, the schoolmaster, the Red Lady and the White Lady, the screaming man...the list goes on and on. There are 16 ghosts in all to make the record books. The place is full to overflowing with all kinds of specters.

No matter where you are in Pluckley, there is almost always something ghostly nearby. It may be a strange noise, or perhaps it is a glimpse to tantalize the peripheral vision, but there is usually *something*. The most common experience, seen as recently as the mid-1990s, is the phantom coach and horses that travel around Pluckley's various roads and lanes. The spectral carriage has been spotted on the road to Maltman's Hill, and there are reports of it rolling through the village and traveling along the roads on the other side of Pluckley. Witness accounts generally describe a four-wheeled coach and two horses, though the occasional person sees a single horse pulling a two-wheeled carriage. One couple clearly saw a horse-drawn carriage being pulled up the hill by Pinnock's Crossroads away from them on a recent October evening. Another sighting happened on the village's back roads when the son of a resident was making his way home. The horse and coach passed right by him, which he reported when he got home as an amusing tale, not realizing he had seen a ghost. In November 1997 another visitor to the village reported hearing the very loud sound of hooves on cobbled street from within his car.

The really odd thing is that no one knows where the spooky coach originated, so there is no sense of where it came from or where it is going. It appears so often that it doesn't seem likely that it is a lost soul wandering without purpose. Could it simply be what is sometimes called a "replay ghost"—"a hologram acting out its role in the great cinema of time," as London archeologist Dr. R.C.C. Clay put it. In other words, perhaps the coach and horses are merely an imprint that was left on the Pluckley landscape to replay at certain times ad infinitum. Or the coach and horses may be spirits from another place. While most places have only homegrown ghosts, more or less clearly identifiable through history, this village—or is it its people?—seems to attract all kinds of specters.

There is the unnamed ghost of an 18th-century highwayman, for example, who met a violent death at the end of a sword after a failed attempt to outrun the law. As one version of the legend has it, the thief raced through the village with police in hot pursuit but he lost them at a fork in the road. He hid in a hollowed out oak tree at Frith (aptly pronounced Fright) Corner, but one of the lawmen spotted the villain's horse and quietly sneaked up to the tree where he ran his sword through the highwayman's heart. Other versions say the highwayman put up a fantastic fight but was overpowered and killed. Yet another account states that it was a would-be victim, who had been told to watch out for the man who hid in a tree waiting to rob passersby, that approached with his sword drawn and killed the thief in his lair. Whatever the case, the ghost of the dead robber appears at Frith Corner, sometimes pinned to a phantom tree (the oak tree is no longer there) and slumped over.

There is also the "Watercress Woman"—the ghost of a gypsy who lived on the banks of the Pinnock Stream and earned a pittance selling the watercress that grew there to local residents. Everyone knew her and yet they didn't for she has no name in any history book. The eccentric old woman bided her time smoking and imbibing the gin she kept in a flask. One evening, she either fell asleep while she puffed on her clay pipe or sparks fell onto her gin-soaked clothes. Somehow the fabric caught fire and the gypsy woman died in a ball of flames, her screams of terror and pain unheard by the people of Pluckley. It wasn't until the next day that some-one found her flask and broken clay pipe lying next to a pile of ashes. As if to make a point, the woman's spirit inflicted her agonizing howls on people who happened by the river bank for many years after her death. She also appeared as a bright, flaming apparition. Over time, the Watercress Woman's spirit weakened to become just a faint, pink glow. Some witnesses claim to see her misty figure sitting on the Pinnock Bridge.

There are quite a number of ghosts in Pluckley that are connected to the village history through the Dering family, lords of the manor from the 15th century until World War I. At St. Nicholas church, two female phantoms are said to wander among the gravestones, though neither have been seen or heard for some time. The Red Lady may be another unknown ghost but the more popular notion is that she was a member of the Dering clan whose baby died during childbirth. The child, possibly illegitimate, did not receive an official burial in the family crypt but was quietly and quickly laid to rest in an unmarked grave. The normally detailed Dering family records show no mention of this unfortunate infant or the woman who reputedly died soon after. Her spirit haunts the graveyard, wandering between the tombstones and if you listen you may hear her calling out to her child. Why is she dubbed the Red Lady? That too is part of the mystery. It's unclear whether her ghost is seen wearing red, or if she has a mane of long, red hair; one thing is certain and that is the distinction between her spirit and that of the White Lady.

Also haunting the St. Nicholas cemetery is the ghost of another member of the Dering family, again unnamed other than by the color of the gown her spirit is said to wear. Though her identity is a mystery, most accounts attribute her to be one of the medieval Dering wives, a woman so beautiful that when she died at a young age her heartbroken husband could not bear the thought of what would happen to her when placed underground. To stave off the effects of the grave, he apparently had her swathed in a gorgeous white gown, placed a single red rose on her chest, then had her body encased in a series of airtight lead coffins before being placed in an oak coffin and lowered into the Dering family crypt. Despite such corporeal confinement, the woman's spirit remains quite free. She wanders in the church chapel and out in the yard in her flowing white dress, always carrying the single red rose.

It's worth noting here that there is another ghost at the church. Strange lights have been seen from one of the windows near the Dering Chapel and they often coincide with the sound of rapping from the vault under the floor. The phenomenon was so well known that a paranormal research group asked the rector if they could spend an evening in the church recording whatever they might be able to catch on their array of cameras, audio recording equipment and thermometers. After a relentlessly uneventful evening, the group met with the vicar before leaving to thank him for the opportunity. When he asked how it had gone, they told him it would have been incredibly boring if not for several visits by the vicar's dog. The vicar then told them he did not have a dog.

Over on Bethersden Road, the "Tudor Lady" haunts another of the Dering family homes. Known as Rose Court, the large home is thought to have been built at least 250 years ago for one of the Dering lord's mistresses. The woman supposedly fell in love with a monk who lived across the field at Greystones and when it became clear that her heart's desire would not be fulfilled, she took her own life by drinking a concoction of poisonous ivy and berry juices. Among the various creepy things that occur in the home, people hear strange sighs and groans, and things like clothing and furniture are moved around during the night. Others reported hearing her call for her two dogs between 4 and 5 PM—the time of her death. Skeptics say the sound neatly coincided with feeding time at the nearby kennel and when it moved, the ghostly calls ceased.

It follows then that over at Greystones on Station Road, the large pale gray house is haunted by a lovelorn monk. According to one legend, when the monk heard of the death of his beloved over at Rose Court he became despondent, spending his days walking through the fields and lanes where they had secretly met for romantic trysts. The monk died eventually of a broken heart. Another theory is that he was the lady's confessor in the years that the Roman Catholic religion was banned, forcing them to meet secretly. If true, the monk may have met a tragic end like many Papist monks who lived in England at the time. His shadowy figure has been seen reflected on walls in some of the newer homes along the path he and his lady may have trod. In 1989 an American journalist claims to have seen the very recognizable brown-robed figure moving about behind Greystones.

On Dick Buss' Lane—named after a local miller—one of the school's teachers continues to haunt the people of Pluckley after his awful suicide in the 1920s. No one knows why the man hanged himself from one of the bay laurel trees that lined the road, but his shimmery shape has been seen swinging back and forth in the place where he died. The trees are no longer there, and in fact there is no real record of anyone seeing the schoolteacher's ghost, so this one may fall into the category of "good story to tell children to make sure they don't dawdle on the way home."

The same could be said about the "screaming man," whose ghostly howls send chills up spines. The man worked at the brickworks and apparently fell to his death into one of the site's clay-holes. No official accident report appears in any village record. No one has seen his ghost. But people claim to hear the ghostly echoes of his last terrifying screams as he hurtled headlong into the workings, a sound remarkably similar to the horrible yowls of a vixen echoing across the fields.

Finally, the Blacksmith's Arms and the Black Horse Inn are thriving businesses based in buildings that date back to the 14th century. As such, they come with a few ghosts. The

Blacksmith's Arms originally housed a forge and then became an alehouse. In the late 1990s it became a tea room run by Gloria Atkins. There is no doubt in Gloria's mind that her establishment has at least two spirits—a cavalier that enjoys strutting about the upper-level rooms and a Tudor maid who stands at the fireplace turning the spit. Gloria has had her own encounters with her paranormal guests, watching a row of mugs hanging on wall pegs suddenly start to swing as if someone had run a hand along them. And, one afternoon in 1997, she heard the front door open and close, and then heard a chair in the tea room slide back from a table. She went in to see what the customer wanted, only to find the room empty.

The Black Horse Inn began as a farmhouse surrounded by a deep moat. Now it is a pub with a local reputation as being the home of a ghostly prankster, although the inn is not one of the "official" Pluckley haunts. The unseen trickster makes off with the personal possessions of staff and customers, moves objects in the kitchen and on occasion locks the owner out of her own drinking establishment. Owner Laura Gambling also witnessed a glass slide along the length of a shelf above the bar, stopping just before toppling over the edge. Dogs bark at some invisible entity in the kitchen. And to cap it all off, Laura's daughter says she saw the ghost of a woman wearing a red dress in an upstairs room.

Distinguishing between myth and reality is difficult when it comes to Pluckley's ghosts. Many of the stories have been told and retold for decades, embellished and altered along the way. There are a dozen or so "official" ghost stories that continue to bring visitors looking for a thrill through the area every Halloween. I leave it to you to visit the delightful little community and decide for yourself where the ghosts dwell.

# Quarantine Station
## SYDNEY, NEW SOUTH WALES, AUSTRALIA

If you really can't get enough of ghosts, then here's the place to visit. Not just for a tour, but for an overnight sleepover in the former hospital of Australia's Quarantine Station—the first—and last—point of call for many 19th- and 20th-century travelers. This complex of buildings overlooking Sydney Harbour, which resembles an army barracks more than it does anything else, vies for the title of "most haunted place" on this continent (the other being Monte Cristo house on page 136).

The popular "Sleepover Ghost Tours" resumed in 2005 after a 10-year hiatus. The historic site, now operated by the state parks department, lets visitors spend a night after taking an extensive tour through the most haunted buildings in the complex. Even the press release acknowledges the many specters on the premises, such as the Matron, an Asian man and a little girl with braids. "The Quarantine Station is one of Sydney's most popular tour sites, even though some visitors—and staff—have vowed never to return," said David Thompson, who carries the title Acting Visitor Service Manager and also conducts ghost tours on the site. One staff member who claimed she felt an invisible force try to shove her off a cliff ran from the site without even taking her belongings, and later sent people back to retrieve her things.

The idea behind setting up the station in 1828 over a large section of North Head was to prevent epidemics by stopping ships with infected passengers and keeping those infected

*The only remaining gravestone, shown here, is on top of hundreds of unmarked graves.*

isolated from the general population. It remained Sydney's main line of defense against infectious diseases such as bubonic plague, cholera, smallpox and Spanish influenza for more than a century, closing in 1984. This barrier between the developing colony and the outside world became not only a holding ground, but a massive burial plot. As one might expect, many of those brought to Quarantine Station died of their illnesses; 527 men, women and children are buried in three nearby cemeteries.

Stories of ghosts date back to 1832 when night-shift nurses reported seeing spectral Chinese men wearing traditional clothes and long single braids walking through the hospital wards. Nowadays, the stories are documented by the National Parks and Wildlife Service staff. David Thompson says they keep track of every apparition, cold spot and tap on the shoulder when no one is standing near. "It's uncanny how many of our visitors report seeing apparitions—and just how similar the reports are, even though they're from people who've never met each other," he is quoted as saying in a recent press release. "The most frequently reported sightings are of a traditionally dressed Chinese man, who is often seen near where Asian people were accommodated in the station, and a little girl with plaits who has been linked to a child who went missing on North Head a century ago. Other reports—from visitors and staff alike—include self-slamming doors, and showers and lights coming on even though the water and electricity weren't connected. One guide reported seeing his didgeridoo being scraped back and forth against a wall, apparently all by itself."

A Matron supposedly haunts one of the wards, making life physically uncomfortable for those who dirty the rooms. According to a report done by Rowena Gilbert of Castle of Spirits.com, one fellow judged poorly by making disparaging comments about the cleanliness of one of the bathtubs. Within moments, he felt a huge wave of nausea come over him, forcing him outside to retch.

The shower block houses the most violent ghosts, leading psychics to report a great evil emanating from one of the corners, possibly generated by past sexual abuse. Lights frequently turn themselves on and off, and bulbs have been known to explode during tours. Footsteps and banging noises have also been heard, and on one tour several very frightened women reported that the showers actually started. For the record, there is neither power nor water running to the building.

Not surprisingly, the mortuary generates some of the best stories. Nurses in the 1920s and 1930s used to report the ghost of a sailor standing by a window. Another legend tells of an Aboriginal man whose face somehow became etched onto the window-glass during a severe lightning storm. Although the tour guides will show the window, it takes a little or perhaps a lot of imagination to see the man's face. More terrifying is the story from a woman on a recent ghost tour who saw a corpse lying on the slab. Not a fake one, put there for the tour, but a body that no one else seemed to be able to see. Bad enough, but then the dead man began to speak to her, complaining of what had been done to his body and revealing a deep cut from his naval to his neck.

Shimmering shapes, the sounds of people disembarking ships, feeling someone brush by: these are just some of the incidents listed by visitors. The young girl said to be one of the regular ghosts will tug at people's sleeves or try to hold their hands. One psychic claims she saw the little girl walking through a tour group, staring up at the faces as if trying to pick someone out of the crowd. A sad, lost little soul in search of her parents, perhaps?

A journalist sightseeing through Quarantine Station in 2001 admitted to being fairly skeptical at the outset of the tour. He observed other people having spooky things happen, like feeling something move past when no one was near, but felt that could easily be the power of suggestion—until he reached the mortuary. After the park ranger took them

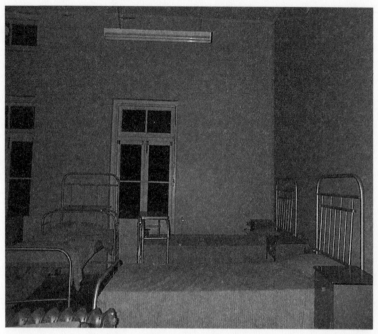

*The hospital ward is known to be haunted by ghosts of patients and nurses.*

through the small space and gave them the lecture, the journalists on the tour were allowed to take turns looking through a large window into the room that had all the lab equipment. He was the last person to lean in for a look and just as he peered into the window, a face popped up and stared back at him. Shocked, he made a loud cry, which he then brushed off by saying he lost his balance and nearly fell. Later, however, when the tour ended, he asked the park ranger if the ghost in the lab was Polynesian. The park ranger looked surprised, but told him that yes, there were reports of a Fijian spirit haunting that room.

The word quarantine originates from the Italian *quaranta*, meaning 40, and harkens back to Jesus' self-imposed exile, spending 40 days in the desert. For many of the detainees who traveled great distances only to become sick on the overcrowded ships, there would be no salvation from the deadly diseases. A visit to Quarantine Station is for the courageous only.

# 6
# Prisons

# Haunted "Hell on Earth"
## Port Arthur, Tasmania

Port Arthur started out in 1830 as a timber station, a small logging camp on a small isthmus on the island of Tasmania isolated from the rest of world by the sea. Three years later, officials recognized its potential as a place to which they could slough off societal detritus and turned it into a male-only prison settlement for hard-core convicts to serve out their sentences. For most of the men sent there, it was a life sentence in the true sense of the word. Forced to work on brutal chain gangs, subjected to regular floggings, fed poorly and treated like animals, many prisoners died within Port Arthur's walls. Now it is a major tourist site that offers ghost tours because—surprise, surprise—the old prison is quite haunted. Sightings of ghostly prisoners walking in the former exercise yard, weird glowing lights on video recordings, cold spots and oppressive feelings of evil are just a few of the paranormal phenomena recorded recently in the place nicknamed by the prisoners as "hell on earth."

To say the prison overseers broke men's spirits would be classic understatement. According to various reports, the penal settlement that ran until 1877 took men and wrung them out. Prisoners shipped there for crimes as menial as petty theft came from as far away as Ireland, England and Scotland and those who survived the journey knew they had almost no chance of ever seeing their homes again because they had no way to earn the return fare. The inmates were essentially slave labor for the timber industry, working in chain gangs to haul heavy, back-breaking logs. Many men were also confined to small pens and forced to manually break stones for making bricks. Any attempt to escape resulted in 100 lashes, publicly meted out for the rest of the inmate population to see. A separate prison was built and prison officials adopted the practice of punishing prisoners by putting them in isolation, which meant being locked in a small, unlit, sound-proof cell. Many convicts simply went mad from the unrelenting abuse, sometimes killing other inmates or taking their own lives. Others died from disease, getting fatal infections from sores caused by the chains or scurvy from the diet of only salted meat. Suffice it to say that when the prison closed, and even after it was gutted by fire, the tormented souls of dead prisoners remained.

Ironically, the convict settlement attracted tourists as early as the 1920s. People flocked to see the horror of life at the prison. Eventually, it was taken over by the Port Arthur Historic Site Management Authority and the buildings are bona fide historic sites with all that entails—brochures, ghost tours and, of course, tour guides. One of the ghost tour operators, Todd Darling, participated in a broadcast about his experiences in November 2004 and told a local television station that in more than 1000 tours he has had several strange experiences ranging from hearing odd noises to feelings of being followed to seeing actual apparitions. "I've seen three ghosts," he told the ABC TV crew. One of the weirdest stories he relates didn't happen to him, but to some tourists who were on his tour. A husband and wife were using a night-vision video camera to record inside the prison. While they were on the tour they didn't notice anything strange, but they returned to the tour office the next day with the tape. The husband announced he didn't believe in ghosts, and wanted an explanation for what was on his videotape. Everyone in the office who looked at it was equally surprised at what he had captured in his recording. Todd explains, "The actual husband is filming away, he pans past his wife…and you see just this glowing mist that separates from her body and drifts down the corridor." Tourists who witness ghosts or have other bizarre things happen are asked to fill out an "unusual occurrence form," which goes in a binder so the staff can keep track of the stories. Todd Darling says their record alone is confirmation of the ghosts at the prison. "You've got to wonder how is it that people who are strangers, who don't know the story, from different places in the world, have come and seen the exact same thing 10 years apart."

Among the other stories in Todd's repertoire of ghoulish goings-on is the ghost of a woman believed to have been the wife of one of the jail staff. Though largely myth, the tale has it that the woman died giving birth. Her sad, sobbing spirit haunts the parsonage and one of the houses on the grounds. It may be only a tall tale, but there is at least one child who believes it for truth. While touring the house, the toddler apparently asked to be let down from his mother's arms and ran the length of the veranda to throw his arms up as if someone would pick him up. When asked why he did that, the child replied that the lady who lived there would like to play.

There is also the story of the phantom footsteps in the junior medical officer's house. The floors had been sanded and refinished, the doors locked to let the varnish dry, and the next morning the contractors returned to find two imprints—an adult footprint and a smaller child's footprint—clearly visible on the new surface. There was no explanation for how those single marks could have been made—no one had entered the home overnight and it would be hard to leave just one blotch. Were the ghosts treating the new floor like fresh city sidewalk cement—playing a game to mark their territory?

Other witnesses claim to have seen inmates walking in the courtyard. One man on a tour with his wife thought he was seeing things until his partner told him she could also see a gray figure walking back and forth in the corner of the yard. Several other people on the tour also observed the apparition. Rowena Gilbert of Castle of Spirits.com says there are also reports of black shadows, ghosts of officers, disembodied footsteps, and strange lights that float over the grounds and travel in and out of buildings. She rates it as number one on a top 10 list of haunted places in Australia. It is definitely worth a look if you are in that part of the world—even if you don't see anything spooky, it is a good reminder of why human rights remain a paramount issue of our time.

# Oakalla Prison Phantoms
## BURNABY, BRITISH COLUMBIA, CANADA

Prisons have their own particular brand of energy—darker, ominous, repressed. Not surprising, given the conditions. The Oakalla Prison Farm in Burnaby, British Columbia, deserves special mention because within its walls, more than 40 inmates were executed—hanged by the neck until dead. Some of those dead prisoners may not have found peace and freedom beyond the mortal coil. One former employee of the corrections system is quite sure that at least one convict's spirit remained trapped behind bars.

Leigh Ondrack worked as the business manager for Prince George, British Columbia's correctional center in the early 1990s. Right about that time, Oakalla was being shut down. The prison, which had opened in 1912, was originally designed to house a maximum of 484 prisoners, but its population often numbered well over 1000. The overcrowding issue resulted in three new corrections facilities, and the old prison closed on June 30, 1991. Up in Prince George, Leigh saw an opportunity to get some desperately needed furnishings and supplies from Oakalla for his center, so he drove down with a truck and made arrangements to haul away some of the surplus furniture and equipment. "It was my job to ship these items back up to our facility," Leigh explains.

"One day, I had to go back to a Quonset hut that was being used as a storage room. When I unlocked the door, I heard footsteps on the second floor," recalls Leigh. He knew he had the only key to the building and the door had been locked. Given the building's design—it looks like a long tunnel, with a rounded roof and concrete floors—there was no other way to get in. The security people at Oakalla had told him they were having problems with people breaking into some buildings looking for souvenirs. "So I assumed I had caught someone in the act."

Leigh went upstairs to confront the person, but didn't see anyone. "I checked every nook and cranny up there and kept an eye on the stairs, which were the only way down." After a thorough search, Leigh realized he was alone on the second floor. He suddenly had a strange feeling in the pit of his stomach. "I was constantly glancing around, nervous."

He started back down the stairs. "Just then, I felt the hairs on the back of my neck rising and I distinctly felt that someone was watching me. I whirled around but there was no one there." Leigh didn't wait to find out more. He rushed out and locked the door.

Later, in the safety of his Prince George office, Leigh told one of the former guards who used to work at Oakalla about his experience. "He told me that, over the years, guards had reported strange phenomena at the jail. It was rumored that the ghosts of everyone who was ever executed there still walked the grounds of the prison."

If that were true, there would have been quite a cadre of imprisoned incorporeal beings. From 1919 until the abolition of the death penalty in 1959, 44 prisoners were executed by hanging on the Oakalla site. The first execution was that of 25-year-old Alex Ignace on August 29, 1919. Leo Mantha was the last prisoner executed, on April 28, 1959. In 1936 there were several double hangings and even one triple hanging. Leigh Ondrack feels he may have met the ghost of one of the slain men. "It's the strangest thing I experienced," says Leigh.

As an aside, Leigh knows what he speaks of when it comes to paranormal phenomena. He has a list of eerie and unexplainable incidents that date back to his first marriage and honeymoon on Vancouver Island in 1969. He and his bride were wandering about Victoria's Butchart Gardens when they encountered the spirit of Jennie Butchart, who apparently loved her gardens so much she still wanders through them. Years later, Leigh and his current wife were unpacking after moving into a home in Prince George. His wife had gone out and he was alone in the house; Leigh heard the front door open and shut, but when he checked, no one had entered the house and the door was locked. Soon after, he got up one night to get a drink and bumped into what he thought at first was his wife in the hall. He mumbled an apology, then realized it was not his wife at all, but merely the shape of a woman whose face he couldn't make out.

As for Oakalla, after the prison was torn down, developers moved in and built condominiums and town homes on the site. Leigh told me he had been told that some of the new owners felt the presence of a friendly ghost in an area where the prison's entry stairway had been. The ghost is presumed to be that of a former guard who passed away, but didn't pass on to the other side and continues to keep watch. I was unable to confirm that story; however, I was told that nothing of the prison's physical structure remains. It was leveled to the ground. Perhaps felling the prison walls allowed those spirits who remained locked on earth's plane to go freely on to the spirit realm. And perhaps not. It would be interesting to survey those living on the old prison site to see if they have encountered anything odd.

# The Old Melbourne Gaol
## MELBOURNE, VICTORIA, AUSTRALIA

How about a game of word association? Say, 19th-century prisons. For me, I think grim, dark, death. That was certainly the case in Melbourne, Australia, where its overcrowded jail saw 135 inmates hanged and dozens more subjected to harsh punishments. Is it any wonder Melbourne's former penal center—now a museum—is haunted by many of the tormented souls who suffered and died behind the dense stone walls?

Built in the mid-1800s, the Old Melbourne Gaol still holds mementos of severe restraint and punishment to remind modern-day visitors how difficult life would have been for those found guilty and incarcerated. It's interesting to note that the jail modeled itself on England's Pentonville Prison and was considered to employ the latest, up-to-date methods of prisoner reform. However, the issues of overcrowding were never solved and a review of the system in 1870 resulted in recommendations of closure. It didn't officially shut down until 1929. During World War II it was used briefly by the Americans as a military prison. After that, the Victorian Police Force stored equipment in it until the National Trust of Australia finally acquired it and turned it into a public museum.

Outlaw bushranger Ned Kelly is the most famous prisoner listed on the jail records. Kelly was captured in the infamous shootout at Glenrowan in 1880 where the rest of the "Kelly Gang" died in a hail of police bullets. After a two-day trial, a judge found the 25-year-old Kelly guilty, and he died at the

*The Old Gaol is ranked as one of Melbourne's most haunted sites.*

end of a hangman's rope in November 1880. Many people assume his spirit is one of the ghosts at the jail—a natural enough assumption given that his death mask and armor from the shootout are on prominent display. But most paranormal experts say that because his remains were moved to the Pentridge Prison, Kelly's ghost does not haunt the building. If it isn't Ned Kelly's ghost that wanders about, then whose is it? Some believe that at least one of the phantoms is that of a former female prisoner. Many visitors sense a chill when walking down the narrow corridor between the three levels of cells. Cold spots have definitely been noted in particular cells and there have been several sightings of ghostly apparitions. The most recent occurred during a frightening vigil by local paranormal researchers.

Darren Done headed the team of six who bravely spent the night on a paranormal watch in February 2005. They arrived on a Saturday night prepared to stay awake and record any unusual happenings. Done has conducted many such missions, approaching his work with skepticism and an appreciation for the power of suggestion. "The aim of the team I work with is to try and rationalize alleged paranormal events," he told an Australian radio station. "I rely more on our equipment than on our own senses." But on this night his eyes would witness something quite chilling.

Upon arriving, Done and his team got busy preparing to record anything that might transpire. "We set up huge amounts of equipment all around the location—things like night-vision cameras, motion-sensing cameras, passive alarm systems and laser-guided digital thermometers. And during the course of Saturday night we had five members of the general public sitting around an area of monitors which were all giving audio and video feeds from one of the areas we were covering." Ironically, all that technology failed to record the night's big event. All six people suddenly saw an unexplained light move along one of the jail walkways. It stunned the group. "For around about eight seconds there was a point of light which gave the appearance of somebody carrying a candle. That's what it actually looked like, a candle flame moving across one of the walkways in the jail. It was very, very noticeable." The cameras did not catch the moving light because they had been set up at the other end of the jail where Done thought there would be a lot of activity. "It's just really disappointing," he says. The group tried to find some explanation for the strange light, but could not find any possible rationale other than the obvious—they saw a ghost. The team also discovered later that they had taken several photographs with mysterious orbs of light throughout the jail.

It wasn't Darren Done's first bizarre experience at the Old Melbourne Gaol. On his first expedition in the very early hours of June 21, 2003, his team heard a woman cry out for help. "We not only heard a female voice but we actually did record it on some of the equipment in there," says Done. "We went back to the management of the jail with this result and they said it was absolutely impossible because there were no female prisoners kept in this part of the jail." Done asked the manager to do some more research and he received a call a couple of days later. The manager was very excited about what he discovered. "He found a female prisoner who had been kept in there in 1865 who had committed suicide on June 21, on the exact same date as our visit." The woman, known as Lucy R., died 138 years prior to the ghost-hunting team's visit, yet her voice rang out clearly on the tape.

The following year, Done and his team returned on the anniversary of the woman's death, and at the end of the night thought nothing had happened. However, when they reviewed the digital videotapes, they had recorded a woman's voice ordering them to leave. He recalls, "You can hear us saying it was time to pack up, and at that same point a really strong female voice came right over the top of us saying "Get out!" And everyone who has heard that voice can even pick an accent out of it. It sounds like a German accent."

Others who visit the jail pick up from some of the cells a strong energy that almost acts like a barrier, preventing them from entering the space. Rowena Gilbert of Castle of Spirits.com and the Australian Ghost Hunters Society says she visited the cell next to the gallows where prisoners spent their last hours before being executed. Gilbert immediately noticed a strange feel to the whole building and honed in on an overwhelming sense of sadness in the cell of the condemned. "The cell reeks of fear and terror," she reported on her web site.

The Old Gaol is ranked as one of Melbourne's most haunted sites—hardly surprising given all the recent sightings. Who is the spirit carrying the candle? A night watchman on permanent rounds? It is rumored that one of the hangmen killed himself to avoid having to hang a female inmate slated for execution. Could he still be wandering through the bluestone building, unable to forgive himself for the many lives he assisted in taking?

# 7
# Pubs
# & Restaurants

# Dick Whittington's Pub
## GLOUCESTER, GLOUCESTERSHIRE, ENGLAND

*Whoe'er has travelled life's dull road,*
*Where'er his stages may have been,*
*May sigh to think he still has found*
*The warmest welcome at an inn.*
—William Shenstone (1714–63)

A trip to Gloucester's historic Dick Whittington's tavern is definitely not dull. If the ghosts don't get you, the moving furniture will. Now you may be thinking that the bizarre tales are nothing a sober second trip couldn't fix, but the current owners say nay. According to landlord Rob Owen, his 600-year-old building is haunted, plain and simple. Between the furniture that shifted on its own and the hunchbacked figure seen in the basement, he and his staff are convinced they have a pub full of not-so-peaceful phantoms.

The 15th-century building cites a prestigious pedigree. According to the local preservation trust—Gloucester Historic Buildings Ltd.—the townhouse did originally belong to the Whittington family. The pub's namesake spawned a lengthy and often exaggerated legend about his trip to the big city of London with his cat in 1350 to seek fame and fortune. As the story goes, Dick Whittington buckled when he saw the city from Highgate Hill and was on the verge of taking his feline companion home when the peals of London's bells assailed him. "Turn again, Dick Whittington, three times Lord Mayor of London," is what he apparently heard amid the chimes. So he continued on to London where he became a mercer (a merchant of expensive cloth) and did fulfill the bells' prophesy of becoming Lord Mayor three times. Dick Whittington's image lives on in a statue (holding the cat that does not have any historical evidence to support its existence) in Whittington Park. But does his ghost persist in the pub that bears his name?

No, say historians. The man has been immortalized by modern pantomimes but he died long before the tavern was built. Whose spirit is it then? Rob Owen doesn't know. What he is sure of is that his drinking establishment has seen a fair bit of recent paranormal activity. He told a local newspaper in February 2005 of a very strange happening not long ago. Rob had been worried that people might be stealing from the cellar bar; he asked the barman to create a barricade using stacked chairs to block the doors. "He came back up and told me that he had done it and headed off home," reported Rob. But when he checked up on the chairs later, they no longer blocked the door. Somehow, someone or something had taken them down.

In addition to the mysterious moving furniture, visitors to the bar have noticed orbs—spheres of light thought to be proof of spiritual presence by believers, or simple refractions of light caused by dust flecks by skeptics—on photographs taken in the bar. The spots of light appear above an area that used to be the favorite seat of a recently deceased regular. And Rob's daughter Deborah claims she saw a hunchbacked figure moving about down in the cellar, which then disappeared. Could it be that the dearly departed soul helped out his still swilling buddies by moving the chairs out of the way?

There may be an answer forthcoming, although it wasn't available at the time of this writing. Given the amount of ghostly goings-on, Rob Owen decided to call in a newly formed group of local ghost hunters—the Paranormal Investigation Research Team—to track down the spirits and find out who haunts the Westgate Street bar. The *Western Daily Press* claims the street is one of the most haunted in Gloucester. Just down the way, the Old Crown Inn and the former Theatre Royal both are believed to have ghosts on site. Near the Cathedral, a memorial stands in honor of Bishop John Hooper who was burned at the stake in 1555 for his Protestant beliefs. The ghost of Queen Mary, the monarch who ordered the bishop's execution, supposedly haunts the large, old Tudor building across from the martyr's memorial.

Perhaps the ghosts just take up residence in the nearest available venue as they make their eternal way down the thoroughfare, or maybe there is a spirit trapped in Dick Whittington's that the ghostbusters can identify and assist on its way to the next plane. The next time you are in the neighborhood, be sure to stop by for a pint to find out.

# The Greyhound Inn
## LINGFIELD, SURREY, ENGLAND

Meanwhile, in the large (albeit slightly isolated) village of Lingfield in southeastern Surrey, the owner of the Greyhound Inn struggles to get his ghouls to behave. Staff at the Plaistow Street pub say they have noticed sudden changes in temperature, heard strange noises, witnessed light bulbs explode and even beer barrels being moved. There is a distinct cold spot by the fireplace and there have been several sightings of the ghost of a young girl who was apparently burned there. Manager Paul Edkins was frustrated by the weird happenings within his walls. He is quoted in an interview saying, "I just want to know what it is. It's really hard to put your finger on what is happening, but there is definitely something there."

In the fall of 2004, Mr. Edkins called upon the UK Paranormal team to investigate the bizarre goings-on at his well-known watering hole. The site has been in use since 1584, and the pub was formerly a coaching inn. One of the pub's main attractions is an old circular skittle room (a British form of ninepins, in which a wooden ball is used to knock down the pins) with a secret room in the back. Local smugglers allegedly used the small, hidden room for covert meetings. There is also an archway visible in one of the cellar's brick walls; it is rumored that the archway used to be the entrance to a tunnel that leads to a nearby church. The paranormal team held an investigative silent vigil in September 2004, and while they had some interesting experiences, they did not solve the problem by any means. They did report that after sitting for several hours in various places inside the pub that they felt sure there are active spirits on the premises: a young boy and a man. They just didn't get anything concrete about who the spirits are or why they are haunting this pub. The report states, "We all got the impression that whatever it was wanted us to know it was there, but was very good at eluding or hiding itself, only giving us small teasing glimpses." Those teasing glimpses took the form of pokes and prods felt by the paranormal team members. One woman felt a tap on her shoulder and another felt herself pulled toward a wall.

This recent investigation does support the claim of Eddie Pratt who visited the Greyhound in 1976 and, while touring through with then owner John Chapman, claimed to see a young boy of about eight wearing a 19th-century-style gray suit with a white collar. Mr. Pratt saw the figure in the skittle room; John Chapman felt a sharp chill that made him shiver but did not see anything. The Chapmans, like Paul Edkins, were intrigued by their employees' reports that the place had ghosts. The kitchen help reported that small utensils kept vanishing and some people said invisible hands touched them. That might not have been enough to warrant a claim of "haunted," but on top of that the Chapmans' dog snarled, snapped and got downright vicious when forced to go near the cellar door or the stairs leading below.

Which brings us back to the current investigation. Since the UK Paranormal team confirmed the presence of a young boy, coordinator Jo Holness reported, "We all felt it would be a good idea to return to the inn at a later date with a medium to see if we could determine more about what or who this elusive presence was." She has booked a medium for a return visit, but had not gone back at the time of this writing.

# Visiting the Wheatsheaf
## THORNTON HEATH, SURREY, ENGLAND

When a ghost greets a team of ghostbusters with a polite "hello," you have to know it feels pretty secure in its environment. In this particular instance, the socially well-adjusted phantom dwells in the Wheatsheaf Inn in Thornton Heath, which lies south of Norbury. UK Paranormal Investigations discovered during their night inspecting the premises that some of the baffling and bizarre experiences of those who work at the inn have a predictable explanation: the place is quite haunted.

The Wheatsheaf Inn's history certainly lends itself to ghost lore. Though you would never know it now, there used to be a pond in Thornton Heath and the large area near the pub was quite isolated, so it became a favorite spot of pickpockets and highwaymen. The pub, back in the 18th century, was a coaching inn where travelers could rest and recuperate from the rigors of horse-drawn treks. Naturally, the nimble-fingered and fleet-footed bandits appreciated having a source of income so readily accessible. As a form of visual deterrence, a gallows was built across the pond (giving it the name Gallows Green) and many a criminal was hanged there. The top floor of the inn served as the court where the felons were convicted and sentenced to die. But that is only one possible source of the inn's ghosts. Locals say the daughter of a previous owner, many generations ago now, was brutally murdered on her wedding day and her killer tried to hide the evil deed by dumping her body into the pond.

Landlady Maria Seal called for help after a burst of strange activity involving bottles moving on their own, glasses falling off shelves and a boiler room that is freezing cold. The team of investigators arrived fully armed to do "technical battle" with whatever spirits might dwell in the Wheatsheaf. Jack Bryer and his gang set up night-vision camcorders, tape recorders and digital cameras in various parts of the pub and in less than an hour they had enough material on tape to convince them that there is a *lot* of ghostly activity. Mr. Bryer told the *Croydon Guardian* in May 2004 that the group focused on the area of the pub that used to be the courtroom and on the current boiler room, which is where those on trial were held. "We set up the camcorder and tape recorder for 45 minutes and when we reviewed it there was a very faint voice which said 'hello.' " In the team's report, they note that many orbs—spots of light believed to represent the presence of spirit energy—could be seen on the tape recorded by their cameras. Then they expanded the search to the basement where "things started to get more active. Orbs began showing up amongst us, and then we all heard a noise that sounded like a box being scraped along the floor, the camcorder even picked the sound up." Back up in the boiler room, they encountered more spooky activity. This time the orbs actually took direction, moving in circles around the head of one of the team members. Jack Bryer couldn't believe his eyes when he watched the video recording. "I asked the spirit to do it a couple of times and each time the orbs moved. This is the first time I've seen orbs move like that. I'm sure the pub is haunted." Buoyed by their success, UK Paranormal Investigations returned for a second night and encountered a veritable flurry of orbs. They also took a digital photograph that they feel captures the wispy image of a man wearing a hat. Is it a smudge on their lens or the real thing? You should check out the web site and decide for yourself.

Landlady Maria is now convinced her inn has a paranormal population. She told a reporter for the *Croydon Guardian*, "I watched the recordings and it's just unbelievable." Unlike some of the other people in this book, she is less inclined to try to get rid of them. "I've been here for four years and if something scary was going to happen I think it would have by now."

# The Castleview Pub
## AYRSHIRE, SCOTLAND

It's tempting to write off the wraith at this Scottish pub near Dundonald Castle in Ayrshire as nothing more than tales of rowdy excess, except that even the owner is fed up with the ghost and called in a team of ghostbusters to help. Terry Quinn's employees complain of being accosted by phantom fingers that pinch their bums while they work. An 18-year-old waitress refuses to use the washroom for fear of running into the ghost. In an interview in December 2004, Tiffany Luxton told *The Sunday Mail*, "It's as if you're being stalked. You feel him brushing past you and touching you. It's really quite scary. You can hear footsteps but nobody is there."

A dozen large water jugs flew off a solid wooden shelf and smashed to pieces. Kitchen workers hear noises when there is no one else nearby. The carbon dioxide used to power the beer lines mysteriously shuts off. Finally, Quinn felt quite fed up with it all and called in the Dunfermline Paranormal Research Fellowship. This newly formed group based in Fife, Scotland is the same one that investigated Dundonald Castle and found enough evidence to proclaim it to be haunted. The investigation has yet to take place (at the time of this writing), but team leader Raymond Crannage believes the Castleview may be suffering from the unhappy spiritual presence of a former owner, since the activity worsened during a period of renovations and changes made to the interior of the pub. Could it be that even in death we resist change?

# Culcreuch Castle
## STIRLINGSHIRE, SCOTLAND

At the bar in Scotland's oldest inhabited castle, Culcreuch Castle in Stirlingshire, there is a spooky song-loving specter. This ancient seat of the Clan Galbraith sits exactly where it always has for the last 685 years at the foot of the Fintry Hills. And as the home of one of Scotland's most aggressive, warring families, Culcreuch Castle has seen no shortage of bloodshed and violence. Surprisingly, the ghosts that haunt this massive stone structure seem relatively benign. There's a female harp-playing spirit and a pushy gray shadow seen moving past people. But it was the jukebox junkie with a taste for very loud Robbie Williams songs that forced owner Andrew Haslam to call in the experts at finding out about ghosts.

If you happen to be passing Culcreuch Castle and catch wind of Williams' tunes like "Angels" or "Rock DJ," it's more than likely a moment brought to you by the problem ghost. Andrew Haslam claims the music is normally kept at a reasonable level, but lately it suddenly blasts out of the speakers at full volume without any help from human hands. "It is very spooky," Haslam told the *Sunday Mail* for a December 2004 article. And the menace becomes more brazen. The woman who manages the bar says the ghost copped a little feel of her behind. The staff has heard kegs of beer being dragged across the cellar floor when no one is down there. And someone is busy pacing the floors in the upstairs restaurant after it has been closed. Finally, the sheer number of sightings and strange occurrences tipped the skeptic scale for Mr. Haslam. "The ghost in the bar has been our busiest spook recently. I don't normally believe in this sort of thing but there have been so many reliable sightings you've got to take them seriously."

Enter the Ghostfinders Paranormal Investigators. On December 5, 2004, seven team members led by founder Mark Turner arrived at Culcreuch Castle with a truckload of equipment. If there was a ghost to be found, they weren't going to miss it. They brought with them four digital night-vision camcorders, two analogue camcorders, four EMF meters, five digital still cameras, an infrared thermometer, two-way radios, an infrared motion sensor, dowsing rods, a pendulum, infrared lights, digital voice recorders, and last but not least, analogue voice recorders. And to make a long story short, they found what they were looking for.

Culcreuch Castle "is very rich in paranormal activity," according to the Ghostfinders' report on the mission. They found orbs in the Chinese Bird Room, one of the hotel bedrooms named for its painted wallpaper. They captured more orbs on their cameras in the dining room, where they also recorded the sound of a woman's scream. "No one in the group heard any noise at the time, which seems strange as the scream was notably louder than our voices." But the really *big* find was in the lower bar—the area with the jukebox. During a séance, the investigators connected to an agitated ghost with a message. Mark Turner's report states, "It seemed we were communicating with the spirit of a young boy, whom we believe was wrongly accused of stealing cattle. Thanks to the information given to us by Graeme, the bar manager, we managed to confirm that the boy's name was Eoin Mackay. The responses we were getting were breathtaking. It was very clear that this young boy had a message to give us. It seemed that what he wanted was for us to tell as many people as possible, that he was *innocent*." Mark feels certain the music-loving ghost is that of a 13-year-old boy who had his hand cut off for stealing many centuries ago. So now what? With his story made public, will the ghostly teen keep his five phantom fingers to himself?

# 8
# Roads

# George's Hill

## CALVERTON, NOTTINGHAM, ENGLAND

In the Nottingham village of Calverton, there are ghosts aplenty, and choosing one to include here was hard to do; so I opted for a story that affects both residents and tourists alike because it occurs on the road heading into Calverton. As the children's song suggests, you can't go over it or under it, but must pass through George's Hill when you are driving into the village. Many taxi drivers who know the area well tend to use an alternate route—especially after dark. They don't want to risk running into the black figure that haunts the area and often shows up unexpectedly as a back seat passenger.

According to accounts gathered by the town, one of the most notorious encounters took place in the 1930s when a Calverton resident named Lawrence Bardhill walked home late one night from the Goose Fair. Mr. Bardhill tramped along the dark, rural road without incident until he reached the peak of George's Hill. Coincidentally, as the clock struck 12, Mr. Bardhill found himself no longer alone on his journey. A figure emerged from the shadows and in the darkness, Mr. Bardhill made out that it was wearing a large hood, making any facial features impossible to distinguish with the exception of a large hooked nose. He noticed his silent companion wore a silver chain around its neck but the body was just a shapeless mass. Frightened, Lawrence Bardhill crossed the road to put some distance between him and the unwelcome figure, but the shadowy being glided across the road to follow him. He quickened his pace to the point of running, but the figure easily matched his speed. After sprinting for a quarter of a mile, the hood-wearing shape finally drifted away and Mr. Bardhill arrived home soon after, winded and speechless with terror.

Since then, there have been numerous reports from people driving along the road through George's Hill at night who say they have seen through their rear-view mirror a dark figure in their car. After only a few moments, it disappeared. A young woman named Sarah claims she recently encountered a black-hooded figure while returning home from a night of babysitting. Despite the summer heat, Sarah suddenly felt the temperature in her car "go icy cold," and then felt as if someone was shoving her seat from behind. When she looked in her mirror, she spied the hooded shape of a figure "looking like a monk." Petrified, she kept driving and when she checked again, the figure had vanished.

Another couple shared a bizarre experience in the early 1990s as they drove up George's Hill. There was a bus traveling up the road just as they neared the top of the hill, and the man was amazed to see what appeared to be a pair of legs running across the road between his car and the bus. At first he didn't say anything, but his wife voiced her astonishment, asking if he had seen what she just saw—disembodied legs wearing riding breeches running between the two vehicles.

On nearby George's Lane, the figure that people claim to see sitting in the back of their car is that of an old woman. Of course, long, curving, unlit country lanes make the perfect place for strange shadows and heart-pounding moments of wondering, *did I just see what I think I saw?* Are the ghosts of George's Lane urban myth? Not according to most nearby residents or those taxi drivers who will only use the Woodborough entrance to Calverton after dark.

# Highway Sheila
## DURBAN, KWAZULU-NATAL, SOUTH AFRICA

Every country has its version of the haunted highway ghost. It generally goes something like this: a restless spirit is often seen by motorists in the middle of the road signaling them to stop. If the driver obliges, the hitchhiker either disappears while in the vehicle or leaves something behind and when the driver tries to return it discovers the passenger has been dead for some time. Sound familiar? Well, in the South African city of Durban, officials felt it was high time to intervene after a sudden onslaught of stories from terrified drivers who were victims of a ghost nicknamed "Highway Sheila." In fact, the city brought in a team of specter specialists to drive the highway phantom off the road.

Of course, Highway Sheila tends to stick to a certain section of road near Chatsworth and the tale told most often has it that a man stopped to give the otherworldly traveler a lift one chilly night and lent her his leather jacket. When he dropped her off, he forgot his jacket. The next day, when he returned to her home to pick it up, the woman who answered the door told him Sheila had died many years before. Baffled, the man visited her grave and—you know where this is going, don't you?—he apparently found his jacket draped on her tombstone. It sounds like a standard urban legend, except that in December 2004 there was a rash of incidents involving sightings of the "mysterious Indian woman dressed in black." One couple driving home in the wee hours of a Saturday morning had to swerve sharply to avoid hitting a woman standing in the middle of the road, waving for them to stop. Nirvana Rupnarain told a newspaper that she and her husband saw a tall woman dressed black with long, wild-looking hair standing with her arms outstretched as their car approached. As they moved closer, the woman stepped directly into their path and stared at them with "wild, glowing, almost spooky eyes." Nirvana's husband wrenched the wheel to avoid hitting the woman, who at the same time jumped out of the way. When they stopped the car and looked to see if she was all right, the woman had vanished.

Not content to terrorize the people of Chatsworth, Highway Sheila shifted along the KwaZulu-Natal coast to an area called Redcliffe, where she frightened a woman returning home from picking her son up at a shopping center. Jain Rajpaul saw a woman wearing a black top standing near a gray car parked by the shopping mall but from the waist down there was only a "white glare." The same long, wild hair covered the woman's face and Jain Rajpaul says she "sped off in fear that she might show her face." Several other witnesses near Redcliffe came forward to say they saw the spooky lady as soon as the reports hit local papers. As public fear of running into the roadside specter grew, the KwaZulu-Natal Department of Transport felt compelled to take action to prevent the possibility of serious injury. Department officials decided to work with religious groups and organized a purification prayer to cleanse the roads of what they feel are a type of phantom "road kill"—earthbound spirits still clinging to this plane after tragic accidents or suicides. Bonga Mpofu, who is responsible for Road Safety, arranged a prayer session because his job is to keep South African roads safe to drive.

If a cleansing ritual will get rid of lurking spirits, he's all for it. "We are hoping to pray not only for those who have died on our roads but those who continue to use it every day," he said in an interview with *The Post* about Highway Sheila.

Although some skeptics say the bigger problem involves spirits of another kind—namely alcohol consumed by people behind the wheel, spiritual groups that attended the prayer session are sure the roads hold many negative influences from trapped spirit energy. They claim the roaming roadside ghosts cause problems ranging from minor injuries to major accidents, and it is worth the effort to help them move on to the next plane. Brahmachari Peetambar of the Chinmaya Mission of South Africa says some spirits don't realize they are dead if they died in a sudden traumatic way, but he is certain Highway Sheila and other spirits who died in tragic accidents loiter with questionable intentions. "Sometimes they can even cause harm."

Other experts in the area say the prayer ritual is a nice gesture but not necessary because the spirits that linger in this realm don't have the ability or intention to cause harm. In any event, the question is whether the prayers work to pacify Highway Sheila. That remains to be seen. So if you happen to be driving near Chatsworth and see a black-garbed, wild-eyed woman standing in the middle of the road, perhaps it might be wise to drive carefully around her—then call the authorities to let them know they need stronger prayers.

# Go, Go, Go, Ghost Car!
## CAPE TOWN, WESTERN CAPE,
## SOUTH AFRICA

In the "inanimate ghost" category, most people have heard of ghost ships, but what about a ghost car? Can a four-wheeled hunk of steel be haunted? Stephen King certainly capitalized on that notion with the infamous *Christine*. Now there's a little Renault in the South African city of Cape Town that seems to have a life of its own. The unassuming little four-door Mégane jumped backwards with the engine off and with the handbrake on. And it happened at least twice. Uphill.

For Ian and Mabel Schietekat, there's no question that what they witnessed in November 2004 has them baffled. They own the Roosboom Guest Suites in Helena Heights—a stunningly scenic area overlooking False Bay and the gentle slopes of the Helderberg. Just before 6 AM, they awoke to a massive crash outside their bedroom window. Grabbing their housecoats and slippers, they rushed out to see that the rented Renault that their German guests were using to tour the Cape had jumped backwards several feet, straight through a solid wood fence. The obvious assumption was that would-be robbers bungled an attempted theft by driving the car backwards through the barrier, but when the Schietekats approached the car they could see it was locked, not running, and the emergency handbrake was upward in a locked position. Not only that, there was no evidence of trying to break into the car and the security fence surrounding the guesthouse remained closed. *So,* they all thought, *how did this happen?*

The Schietekats called the police and the officers who arrived were equally confused by the strange car. One officer even stated out loud that a ton of metal simply can't move if it isn't turned on. As if on cue, according to Ian Schietekat, the Renault "suddenly made a type of roaring sound and gave two powerful leaps backward before it, thank heaven, was stopped by a hibiscus tree." Mabel told a local reporter that the second jumping incident caught everyone, including the police officers, by surprise. "The one police officer's eyes were as big as saucers and my daughter said the car was haunted."

The Renault rental agency and various Renault technical experts were consulted and they all say the same thing: it's impossible. Cars simply cannot move by themselves without combustion or gravity, and in this case the vehicle defied both those assertions. A Cape Town mechanic also thinks the answer may lie with the paranormal. "Maybe there were ghosts," Lino Engel suggested of the Mégane. Could it be that Highway Sheila moved off the roads after the purification ceremony (of the previous story) and relocated to sportier surroundings?

# Roadside Wraiths: Scotland's Haunted A75

## DUMFRIESSHIRE, SCOTLAND

Five decades of police reports, missing victims and frightened motorists puts the 15-mile stretch of road from Annan to Gretna Green in Scotland's Dumfriesshire, known as the A75, at the top of the haunted highway list. This incident is not one measly occurrence that people continue to talk about. It is not even one measly ghost reputed to terrorize the roadway. It is a virtual menagerie of specters that have a nasty way of standing right in front of moving cars and either appearing to fall over as if fatally injured or vanishing in a mystifying vapor.

Reports of strange victimless accidents date back to the late 1950s. A truck driver claims a young couple walking with their arms linked crossed in front of his moving vehicle. Convinced he had hit them, the driver stopped and got out to help the injured pair, but they had disappeared. A skeptic might dismiss this event as the reason there are rules limiting time behind the wheel for truckers. But the bizarre bloodless accidents continued.

Midnight, 1962. Two brothers driving near Kinmount encountered not just ghosts, but half their farm, beginning with the hen that looked like it might crash through the windshield but vanished in the split second before impact. Derek and Norman Ferguson barely recovered from that shocking moment when they saw an old woman running toward them, followed by a long-haired man screaming at her, and several animals running after the man—dogs, cats, goats, more hens—all of which disappeared before hitting the car. The men felt a sharp drop in the temperature so they stopped the car, at which point the vehicle began moving back and forth as if rocked by some unseen force. Derek jumped out of the car and the shaking ceased. The Fergusons collected themselves and started out again, only to run straight into a furniture van that disappeared just as it came near. All right, once again cynics could suggest there might be explanations of substances ingested that *may* have contributed to these double visions. However, the list goes on.

There is one report of seeing a "weird" phantom on the section known as the Kinmount straight. A group of women from Eastriggs traveling in the 1970s claimed they saw something spooky. But it is the two incidents in the mid-1990s that are hardest to dismiss. In March 1995, the Millers—Garson and Monica—were driving 60 mph heading east on the A75 near Kinmount when a middle-aged man wearing a Hessian sack on his head suddenly stood in front of their speeding car. The man's arms were reaching toward the car and it looked like he was waving a rag. There was no time to stop—the Millers' car hit the man. Horrified, they stopped and backed up to where they felt sure the man must be lying, but when they got out to look for him they were the only ones on the road. Still sure they had hit someone, the Millers reported the incident to the Annan police department. Two years later, the Annan police station received another report of a missing victim that sounded remarkably similar to the Miller incident.

Donna Maxwell had her two children in the car as she drove home on a clear July evening at about 10 PM from her mother's house in Eastriggs. She later told police she was driving about 50 mph when a man roughly 30 years old wearing a red sweater and dark pants jumped in front of her car. As she told a local newspaper later, "He just stood there, looking sad. I slammed on the brakes." Donna even closed her eyes, bracing herself against the steering wheel for the inevitable thud. It never came. She opened her eyes and stopped the car. There was no young man anywhere to be seen. Convinced she had hit him, Donna contacted the police station to report the accident. A search by police failed to find any signs of an accident—no blood, no torn clothes and definitely no body. Based on Donna's certainty that she had hit someone, police treated the incident like any other traffic accident and released a description of the man to the media a week later. No one came forward with an explanation. However, others did come forward to say they had experienced the same thing or something similar.

Over near Dornock, several people have witnessed the terrifying disappearance of an old woman in a misty cloud. A woman named Margaret Ching reported that she and her fiancé drove to Gretna one night and as they approached Dornock they suddenly saw a crone in Victorian clothes standing in the middle of the road. Margaret shrieked as the car was about to collide with the woman, but instead it passed right through her. At the same time, both Margaret and her partner felt a cold chill shiver through them. Another local man named Jim claims the very same thing happened to him 26 years earlier on the same stretch of road as he was driving his girlfriend home. The old woman materialized out of a sudden mist, and Jim hit the brakes but his car slid right through the apparition.

Of all the stories, the man with no eyes is the creepiest. A woman in Dornock says she saw a man leaning against a wall and when he turned to face her, he had no eyes, just huge, gaping holes. Others in the village, when they heard her story, admitted to seeing the same horrible figure.

Why so many ghosts on this particular stretch of road? The obvious answer is that over the years there have been many fatal accidents, leaving several unsettled spirits to camp out by the asphalt like a band of ghoulish gypsies. Now, just to muddy things up a bit, the Scottish Office plans to improve the A75—thinking the number of accidents may drop with a better road. Locals, however, are very concerned that the digging up of the road will disrupt and may enrage their spirits. Bad enough to have a road full of impromptu phantoms, but there's no telling what might happen if you tear up the patch of pavement they have been calling home for the past five decades. So if you feel like a thrill, a trip down the A75 might be just the trip you're after!

## The UK's Top 10 Terror Trips

The A75 ranked third in a recent survey conducted by Vauxhall Corsa, with the help of ghost hunters across the UK, of Britain's most haunted roads. The three criteria were frequency of sightings, longevity of reports and likelihood that it was a genuine sighting (i.e., corroborative stories). Here's the list they put together of roads you might want to drive during daylight hours—unless you are a thrill-seeker, in which case you should head out on a moonless night for a trip to remember. Listed in order, the scary roads are as follows:

1. Blue Bell Hill, Kent—A phantom bride believed to have died the day before her wedding runs into oncoming cars and vanishes.
2. A616—Stocksbridge Bypass, Yorkshire—Ghostly children and a monk appear here at the site of a former monastery and work pits that employed child laborers.
3. A75—Dumfriesshire, Scotland (see story above).
4. A361—Nunney to Frome, Somerset—A phantom hitch-hiker gets picked up along this road only to disappear.
5. A12—Norfolk, Suffolk, Essex—The "Grey Gray Man" terrorizes motorists, passing right through their vehicles. A disappearing cyclist that rides through cars also haunts this roadway.
6. A15—Ruskington, Lincolnshire—It's either a highwayman or a hermit monk, but the ghost scares drivers in an area known as Hangman's Haunt.
7. A23—London to Brighton—A female phantom with a limp pays no heed to cars as she makes her way across the road. There is also a handless, footless specter that haunts the area.
8. Holt Bridge—Wrexham, Wales—The spine-tingling screams of boys murdered at this spot stop drivers cold and cause locals to call it the "Bridge of Screams."
9. High Street—Prestbury, Gloucestershire—Several ghosts have been seen, including a motorcyclist, a couple of women and most notably, a man in jockey's clothes and cap who leaves the pub and crosses the road but dissolves into a mist before arriving on the other side.
10. A30—Cornwall—A trio of monks in long, brown robes is seen crossing the road and vanishing in a ditch.

# 9
# Theaters

Let's face it, theater people are prone to believing in ghosts. After all, these are the same people that invented the notion that you must NEVER utter the name *MacBeth* while working inside a theater—it's always referred to as "the Scottish play" or "that play"—for fear of having everything go wrong in your production. The theory goes that Shakespeare included actual black magic spells in the incantations of the weird sisters. Those who appear in the play or those who mention the play's name within the confines of a theater risk having these evils brought down on their heads. Maybe the fact that there were disasters connected to the play dating back to its premiere in August 1606 helps to fuel this belief in "the curse" (the boy actor playing Lady MacBeth died on opening night while backstage). The superstition is not so much about doing the play as about naming it. You are not supposed to mention the title in a theater. Just try it, if you don't believe me, and see if you don't find yourself quickly shoved outside and told to turn around three times, spit, curse the worst profanity you can think of at the time and then wait to be let back inside.

In any event, the point is that the theatrical world always seems a little surreal at the best of times. Ghosts, however, do haunt many of the world's theaters. There are simply too many eyewitnesses to write them off as stage trickery. Perhaps it is the nature of some of the people attracted to the stage, dramatic attention-seekers unwilling to bow out gracefully. Or it may simply be that the space sits empty most of the time allowing the ghosts free reign. My colleague Barbara Smith wrote an entire book on North America's haunted theaters, and there are still dozens of stories to tell. I have included a few here, some old and some brand new.

# Dressing Room No. 9
## DUBLIN, IRELAND

The longest running production at Dublin's Olympia Theatre may well be the spook show. The Victorian-style music hall cum theater regularly packs its 1300 seats—plus one. People working in the theater report rattling windows, moving lights and a very unruly poltergeist in an upper dressing room simply labeled No. 9. It seems the phantom at this theater is more than a little frustrated.

Ancient playhouses always seem to have a ghost of one sort or another. The Olympia started out in 1897 as a music hall called the Star of Erin opened by a man named Dan Lowrey. It closed in 1897 and a few months later was reborn as the Empire Palace Theatre. It eventually changed its name to the Olympia. Now, current staff members hear all kinds of strange noises while working backstage. Locked doors are heard to shake violently, taps and knocks come from empty spaces, and one stage designer sitting in dressing room No. 9 came out when one of the windows started to rattle fiercely—only to discover there was no window nearby. On another occasion, a different stage manager walked in the dressing room to find it looking as if an unhappy toddler had thrown a massive tantrum. Clothes were strewn all over the floor, and makeup had been smeared and thrown around. This event happened during a run of a pantomime show—could it be that the ghost simply can't stand that genre of surreal silent performances? Maybe it hit a little too close to home.

A bizarre yellow light hovering a couple of feet off the floor was seen floating outside the dressing room, then it moved into the room and as it passed through the doorway, the door slammed shut. A strange sound like a muffled whisper was also heard at the same time.

An electrician working in the theater heard the sound of someone walking down the stairs from the dressing room, but when he looked, there was no one else around. No one human, that is. He later claimed to feel someone or something move the theater rostrum, tilting the stage platform while he was on it.

Ever since a séance held in the 1960s, the specter's identity is believed to be that of a man killed inside the theater during the Easter Uprising of 1916. The medium who connected to the spirit energy, and apparently had no prior knowledge of the ghostly occurrences, claimed to get a clear impression of the year 1916. Quoted in Raymond Lamond Brown's *Phantoms of the Theatre*, the woman also had a sense that the man haunting the Olympia did not have a history with it and felt trapped. That's why he was behaving in such a disruptive manner. As it turns out, the record shows that during the violence of the uprising, a man suspected of being an IRA member was shot by mistake inside the Olympia. Many paranormal experts say that in the event of a traumatic death, the person's spirit often gets trapped on this plane, sometimes because they simply aren't aware that they have died or because they still feel there are things they need to accomplish. Or maybe the ghost at the Dame Street theater has grown accustomed to the "smell of the grease paint, roar of the crowd," and just likes to shake things up now and then so he feels a part of the production.

# The Mounds Theatre
## St. Paul, Minnesota, USA

When Raeann Ruth first saw the Mounds Theatre on St. Paul's historic Hudson Street, the boarded-up 1920s silent movie hall verged on becoming derelict. Inside, covered in the dust of decades, its seats were stuffed with junk, partly the accumulation of nearly 80 years and partly the scraps from the man who owned it at the time—a collector named George Hardenbergh. Raeann saw past the mess and mould and envisioned renovating the space for her children's group, Portage for Youth. What she didn't spot were the ghosts lurking in the shadows.

George Hardenbergh donated the building to Raeann's cause. "I knew we could not afford to buy it," Ruth said in an interview with the *Pioneer Press*, "so I asked him if he'd give it to us, and he said yes. I almost fell out of the balcony." Then 82, Hardenbergh said after 35 years of sitting on the property, it would be better to see it put to good use rather than plow it under. Now, after spending more than three years cleaning out the cobwebs and creating a fully functioning community theater, Raeann knows without a doubt that there was more to the Mounds Theatre than met her eye. "I sure do know the ghostly residents of the Mounds Theatre," she told me. "I was also part of the initial paranormal team that did the investigations and I have a good number of stories to tell concerning these three entities, which have made the Mounds their permanent home."

There are at least three ghosts living in the Mounds, though some people are convinced the number is higher.

*Mounds Theatre, c. 1945*

There's a little girl, a former usher and a creepy man who hides out in the projection room. The sweet-looking girl, who Raeann and others have seen playing on stage with a rubber ball, may be the result of a very sinister crime. Raeann theorizes, "I personally believed she was murdered in the theater, as we found a little girl's pink dress stuffed in a tube of PVC piping. Now what was that doing in a movie theater? We also found a little girl's slip and shoe." She says that following publication of the story, she received an anonymous call from someone claiming that a child molester used to loiter near the Mounds and may still be alive. "The caller immediately hung up the phone, after passing along that bit of information, so I was never able to really check it out," she adds.

A cuckolded usher haunts the theater, still in his uniform and carrying the flashlight that probably exposed his girlfriend in the arms of another man. It isn't known how the man died, but his spirit remains tied to the place where his heart was broken. He is often heard crying. Raeann says though he is a sad, troubled spirit, he is harmless.

Then there is the ghost in the projection room—"a nasty sort of fellow, who has sent people screaming from the room on more than one occasion," according to Raeann. She related her experience in the projection room when she ventured there one night with three other paranormal investigators to find out more about the spirit. In a story she wrote about the projection room ghost, she said, "He is the only one that we feel could possibly harm us. He hasn't as yet, but one never knows." The group wanted to find out why the man always seemed to be in what Raeann characterized as "a huff." They arrived at dusk one October evening and made their way up the stairs to the projection booth, already feeling a little fearful. When they tried to turn on the light, it had burned out so they resorted to using their flashlights to explore the dusty, musty room filled with the old projectors and equipment from the theater's heyday as a silent movie haven. As they moved through the space, they even found old handbills promoting upcoming films. In the area with the electrical boxes they discovered an old box lying face down, covered with three decades of grime. Raeann says they were all shocked to see it was a legitimate Ouija board—"not just an ordinary Ouija board made by Mattel or Parker Brothers"—which sent chills through the ensemble. Ouija is generally discouraged by paranormal experts because it is believed to open portals for evil spirits to re-enter this plane.

After searching through the room, the four women sat on chairs, prepared to spend the night. They turned off their flashlights; the room blackened so they could not see one another. Raeann sat absorbing every sound, noticing the temperature plummet and feeling herself begin to sweat. Then, she writes, "All at once the four of us heard a noise emanating from behind the metal partition that we had previously examined. The noise appeared to be a man crying. In between the sobbing we could hear him cursing in a most vile manner. I peered through the darkness and in a swirling cloud of mist my eyes fell on a man slumped in the corner behind the partition. At this point his sobbing seemed to cease. He slowly lifted his head from off his knees that he had been tightly clutching, raised his head and stared directly into my eyes. A fear came over me that shook the foundation of my soul. His eyes were black, glittering in their swollen sockets. I could feel his anger welling up inside of him and I knew I was not welcome in the projection booth, nor were the rest of the people sitting beside me."

The women flicked on their flashlights, and then high-tailed it out of the room. Without speaking they hurried out of the theater, and only when safely outside did they all share their experiences. All four had seen the grim ghost, had heard him crying and swearing, and felt sure he intended them harm. Since then, Raeann has seen the ghost peering down from the projection booth, and feels the inflamed, black eyes boring into her. She still wonders why he haunts her theater. "I can only imagine what events led up to his being here," she concluded in her story. "Does he even know that he is dead, or has he committed such heinous crimes that he has been forced to walk in the shadows of the theater forever to atone for his unthinkable acts? We will probably never know the truth."

As for the possibility that there are yet more spirits at the Mounds Theatre, Raeann Ruth says she hasn't seen them but several of the girls in her youth group will only use the bathroom if they go as a group. Some people claim to have seen a shadow move across the restroom, while others swear they have seen an image in the mirror. All the stories will soon be made public because Raeann plans to produce a play for next Halloween, using all of the stories and experiences that people have had at the theater, and as she points out, "there are soooooo many."

# The Phantom "Federici"
## MELBOURNE, VICTORIA, AUSTRALIA

The gravestone in Melbourne, Australia's General Cemetery is simple and easy to miss. It reads only:

Sacred

to

The Memory of

My beloved Husband

FREDERICK BAKER

(Federici)

Born at Florence, Italy 22nd. April 1850

Died 3rd. March 1888

Rest in Peace

Most people walk right past it without realizing this is the marker of quite possibly the most famous theater ghost in the world. Federici did not follow his wife's wishes. He's been quite busy since he died, haunting Melbourne's Princess Theatre and keeping everyone there on their toes.

Now, how is this for tragic theatrical irony? Thirty-eight-year-old opera singer Frederick Baker, known publicly as Federici, is singing the part of Mephistopheles (aka the devil) in Gounod's opera *Faust*. He successfully sings the dramatically intense bass role, pulling off the difficult blend of devilish and suave, but in the opera's finale as the Italian-born Englishman descends through a trapdoor into "hell," he suddenly has a massive heart attack. He died beneath the stage. Almost immediately thereafter and to this day, management,

*Federici continues to attend the Princess Theatre whenever he misses the spotlight.*

actors, technicians and patrons see the well-dressed man sitting in the dress circle or standing on stage.

According to theater lore, Federici could barely contain himself when the production of *Faust* resumed without him. Many of the performers felt sure that he performed alongside his replacement. That matches the experience of Ernest St. Clair, the actor hired to replace Federici. He claimed that a strong pair of hands pushed him back every time he tried to step forward and take a bow at the end of the performance. It would seem that Federici—even in death—was quite unwilling to share the limelight. It may well be that he simply did not know he was dead; the fatal heart attack happened so quickly that the poor man may *still* think the spotlight shines only for him. Given the number of times he has been seen watching other performances, it is more likely that by now he has figured out the truth and continues to hang around because of his love for theater.

As soon as reports of a ghost in the theater surfaced, the owners used the sudden celebrity as a publicity stunt. The sum of £100 was offered to anyone who would cozy up with the ghost alone at night but despite the offer (that was a lot of money in 1888) no one was brave enough to try for the money.

Others stuck working in the theater at night may have inadvertently earned the £100, even if they never collected. A firefighter on duty in the early 1900s was found cowering in the corner, practically speechless with terror. His job had been to use the new "state-of-the-art" alarm to send an hourly signal to the fire station that all was well in the theater. When he failed to report, a team turned up with sirens blaring. There was no fire, but the terrified man told them he had opened a panel in the roof to let in some fresh air, and by the light of the moon he saw a tall man wearing evening clothes and a top hat standing on stage. He could even see the man's face, describing him as having distinguished features.

In 1917 two witnesses simultaneously stared dumbstruck at the sight of Federici sitting in the dress circle. According to Rowena Gilbert's Castle of Spirits.com, this is the best-known sighting of Mr. Baker. A fireman (presumably a different one) working late saw the singer sitting in the theater. Rather than run away, the fireman looked for someone else to corroborate his story. He found the theater's wardrobe mistress sewing into the wee hours in preparation for an upcoming production and he asked her if she felt like seeing a ghost. The woman agreed and the two walked back up the stairs to the area by the dress circle. There, in the middle of the second row, sat Federici. Oblivious to his audience, he stared down on the empty stage. Eventually the astonished seamstress and fireman just went back to their respective jobs, leaving the ghost to his musing.

Nowadays, the ghost sightings continue to perk up the various productions. In a recent run of *Phantom of the Opera*, the lead male received an unusual letter from an audience member who claimed she saw Federici standing on stage next to him. People claim to feel something brush by them in the hallways backstage, and one performer putting on make-up watched as a hat inexplicably went flying off the stand on which it was sitting. The owners of the theater enjoy having a ghost and consider him to be good luck, even reserving him a seat in the dress circle on opening night. Good to know when you are buying tickets, should you not wish to rub shoulders with a ghostly theatergoer.

# The Tron Theatre

## GLASGOW, SCOTLAND

There are two little children running about Glasgow's Tron Theatre that the staff is absolutely unable to discipline. Reining in a pair of pint-sized phantoms is not the easiest task. You may feel a tug on the sleeve, or if they are feeling particularly playful, a yank on your hair. Somewhat more disturbing is the recent news gleaned from paranormal investigators that the children may be running scared from another ghostly presence.

The site of today's Tron Theatre has a remarkable place in Glasgow's city history; for nearly five centuries it has served as a place of prayer and a place of execution, a meeting hall, a market, a police station and a theater, and somewhere in there it became haunted. The popular theater at 63 Trongate, with its landmark 16th-century steeple, started out in 1529 as a church. When the Scottish government outlawed Catholicism in 1560, it then morphed to fit the shift toward commerce.

For three centuries, the area was the heart of Glasgow's financial and trade district, which is where the Tron Theatre got its name. A *tron* is the beam used to officially weigh trading goods as they are about to pass through the city gate. Two fires (1577 and 1793) nearly destroyed the entire building, and twice the huge steeple—known locally as the clock tower—survived. For a brief period in the early 19th century, even the police occupied the building. Then the Industrial Revolution, and the onset of grime and pollution from the factories, drove the wealthy merchants west, leaving the East

End to develop a new brand of commerce in the "sin" trades—drinking, dancing and brothels. Penny theaters and music halls also emerged as places for people to enjoy themselves.

Jump ahead past a period that the theater management calls "disuse and shabby obscurity" to the 1980s when the Glasgow Theatre Club took over the building for the staggering rent of £1 per year. The theater blossomed, and after a £5 million redevelopment in 1999, the Tron Theatre and its Victorian Bar certainly live up to the Glasgow Theatre Club's aim "to provide opportunities for local writers and actors, to widen the choice for theatergoers and to make the Tron the most accessible and welcoming venue in Glasgow." Little did they know they would be accessible to the spirits of former occupants from centuries past.

Much of the unusual activity seems to take place in the boiler room. On many occasions after hours, two small children have been seen playing or running around there. They have also been spotted in the auditorium, moving across the seats to the east stairwell. Some witnesses say they have seen the little girl staring out from one of the windows.

Front of house manager Jim Davidson says he has experienced what he believes was one-on-one contact with something supernatural a few times in his years working at the Tron. One evening, for example, he was working late in the box office and had a very strong feeling of being watched. He checked behind but there was no one there. Then, he felt an icy finger run down the back of his neck in a ghostly caress. About a month prior to our interview he had another strange experience as he was locking up the box office for the night. "I realized I had forgotten something, so I went back, unset the alarm, went in and suddenly had the feeling that something wasn't right," says Jim. "I heard a door banging, then I heard really heavy footsteps walking across the black slate floor." The box office, Jim explained, is in a separate building from the theater, joined by a pathway. "Now you need to know I'm completely self-contained over there, the area is not that big and there's nowhere to hide. I kind of shouted, 'Hey guys, I'm still here.' It was a bit creepy." Jim says he still occasionally feels "just a wee tickle of fingers" down the back of his neck as he is locking up. It's nothing to be alarmed about. "I don't get scared. There is nothing evil here," he stated.

Different paranormal investigations suggest there is definitely a collection of ghosts within the Tron, though pinning down who they are has proved to be troublesome. One investigator heard voices coming from the stairwell as if someone was walking up or down and chatting at the same time, but no one was there. Through a séance the investigative team contacted a spirit in the plant room who claimed to be an elder named George Reid from the church. Jim Davidson researched the name and found he used to be an elder with the church. One theory is that he is angry because he can no longer see the pulpit from which he used to issue his readings. George obviously has a lot of time on his hands, because he apparently admitted to having fun scaring the two children in the building. (Could it be that he isn't aware they are ghosts too?) This same group photographed several orbs—which they would have discounted as dust except that they appeared in several different cameras taking images in the same place at the same time.

The Scottish Paranormal Investigators spent a night at the Tron with two psychics and several researchers. The SPI team also had strange experiences in the stairwell, feeling that a little girl brushed past them. One of the psychics was overcome by the need to run and skip between the theater seats. During a séance, they contacted two spirits named Maggie or Margaret and Thomas who claim to be related, buried near the Tron, and both very scared of the man who also haunts the theater.

The investigation piqued the interest of a fellow named Fraser who works behind the Tron bar. Jim Davidson says he asked if he could stay on to watch the proceedings and got quite involved. The next thing Jim knew, a trio composed of SPI researcher David Smith, Fraser and him were holding a small séance in the bar cellar. It started out quietly enough. Then whatever spirit inhabits that space made its presence known. "The temperature dropped," Davidson recalled. "Something grabbed Fraser and was noticeably pulling him back. We were all holding hands and both David and I could feel the force. My muscles were flexed to hold him from falling back." Apparently the experience resulted in an abrupt end to the session. Distraught and somewhat overwrought, Fraser bolted.

There were other notable incidents during the all-night vigil. SPI member Katrina reported: "When the team first entered the Victorian Bar, myself and a few other members were standing opposite the door to the kitchen area discussing the investigation. As we were chatting something on my left caught my eye. The best way I can describe it is that it looked as if someone walked by the kitchen door (inside the kitchen). I saw a dark shadow move from left to right. When

I turned away, I noticed Stephen looking in the same direction. He confirmed that he had seen the same thing. On investigation, no one was found to be in the kitchen."

And, oddly enough, the psychics picked up on a false wall in the boiler room. Stephen Barbour reported, "Then came a voice, which told me lots of different things throughout a 30-minute period. I do remember being told that the wall to my right was fake and that it should be taken away again as it was a church gallery." The wall, according to Jim Davidson, leads through to a crypt and was walled up during one period of renovations because of "something scary" that occurred. According to Jim, when the Glasgow Theatre Club first acquired the building, the manager went down to the basement or crypt area to explore the idea of building there. Measuring the area, the manager felt he was being watched. He ignored it until he finally couldn't stand it any longer and turned around to see for himself what was making him uneasy. Jim told me that no one knows what he saw. He refuses to speak of it. All that *is* known is that he ran frantically up the stairs and ordered the builders to block the entrance off immediately. It has never been opened since. "Amazingly enough, when the SPI came out, as soon as one of the psychics walked into the foyer, he just walked right up to the wall and without knowing it was the entrance to the crypt said he felt an archway and doorway. It was incredible that he walked right up to it."

Many of the Tron's employees could wax on about the strange goings-on in this historic theater and bar. Becky, a bar duty manager in the Victorian Bar, had the weirdest Sunday shift on record. During a jazz performance, she heard a hissing sound that kept distracting her. She looked around for its source several times, never spotting anything. "I thought that it was probably feedback from the speakers the band were using, or the coffee machine. But the coffee machine was switched off and on the left hand side, and the band had just gone to a quiet part in the sound." The hissing intensified, became louder, and finally she heard the word, *No.* She knew that she was the only person who heard this as the rest of the room focused on the music. "I kept moving around the bar, just to see if it was where I was standing, but the voice/hissing followed me everywhere and stayed about 3–4 inches away from my right ear." Suddenly, something whacked her on the back of the legs so hard that she fell. The voice disappeared. She looked around as she picked herself up off the floor, but there was no one near enough to have knocked her legs out from under her. Her customers gave her odd looks and she has yet to even the score with that aggressive ghost.

Malcolm, the technical manager, got a little push as well as he worked on the lighting grid above the stage. As he worked, he noticed that the grid started moving as if someone was jumping on it. He turned around to look for the culprit; there was no one there but the movement stopped. And Pat, "one of our finance people," as Jim puts it, works the early morning shift often counting the money from the previous night. She is one of the first people in and she works in an office at the dead end of a corridor. Jim says she often complains of hearing footsteps and she would look because she has cash in her office, but there is never anyone there.

Aside from George the church elder, Jim has done some research and may have a few possible ideas as to where the other souls trapped in his theater came from. "I found out that there was a Glasgow Medical Missonary Society which had a hospital as part of its mandate." The Society's mission when the first hospital opened in May 1867 was "to carry on medical mission work among the poor in Glasgow." For one year the hospital facility operated at Trongate. Jim points out it wasn't right on the site but was close enough to be relevant. He thinks it is very possible two children, siblings, may have died at the hospital and they are the two spirits that continue to startle staff in the Tron.

There was a graveyard in the area as well filled with pauper's graves. The bodies of men sentenced to hang were interred there. Before they died, the condemned men used to be held in the church and were taken through a tunnel to be hanged. Jim says a lot of them died in the tunnel of heart failure, unable to withstand the stress of their pending execution. Local lore says that many of the bodies were disturbed when a large section of the graveyard collapsed on workers building a tunnel for the Argyll Railway at the turn of the 20th century. As they tunneled, the roof fell in and so did the bones of the buried.

Then there is the fire of 1793 set by the infamous Hellfire Club. The notorious gang members met at the Tron churchyard and blew their bugles to wake the dead. Failing miserably and finding themselves cold and soon to be sober, they moved into the session house of the church to thaw out by the fire. Spurred on by more booze, the group decided to test their name and see if they could withstand the fires of hell. Once again, they failed and many of them went down quite literally in flames. Some fled but others including the night watchman died in the fire. A hooded figure has been seen many times walking at the back of the restaurant area (formerly the session house) and Jim thinks that most probably it is a deceased member of the Hellfire Club or the night watchman...although he admits it may also be one of the many condemned souls whose bodies fell into the railway tunnel, which still runs beneath the Tron.

For a night of supernatural shenanigans, make your way to Glasgow. If the scotch doesn't get you, the ghosts will.

# The End